HOW
not
TO SAY MASS

A Guidebook for All
Concerned about Authentic Worship

DENNIS C. SMOLARSKI, S.J.

PAULIST PRESS
New York/Mahwah

Imprimi Potest
November 12, 1985
Very Rev. Paul F. Belcher, S.J. Provincial for Education
California Province, Society of Jesus

The Publisher gratefully acknowledges the permission of the International Commission on English in the Liturgy (ICEL) for the use of excerpts from *The Introduction to the Lectionary, A General Instruction on the Roman Missal, The Sacramentary, Pastoral Care of the Sick, Environment and Art in Catholic Worship*, and *Music in Catholic Worship*.

Excerpts from the Introduction to the Lectionary for Mass from the *Lectionary for Mass* (Second *Editio Typica*) © 1981, International Committee on English in the Liturgy, Inc. (ICEL); excerpts from the English translation of the General Instruction of the Roman Missal from *Documents on the Liturgy: 1963–1979, Conciliar, Papal, and Curial Texts* © 1982, ICEL; excerpts from the English translation of *Pastoral Care of the Sick: Rites of Anointing and Viaticum* © 1982, ICEL. All rights reserved. *Metrical translations of the Song of Farewell* from the Rite of Christian Burial, copyright © 1981, Dennis C. Smolarski, S.J. All rights reserved.

Library of Congress Cataloging-in-Publication Data

Smolarski, Dennis Chester, 1947–
    How not to say Mass.

    Bibliography: p.
    1. Mass—Celebration.   2. Catholic Church—Liturgy.
I. Title.
BX2230.5.S66   1986   264'.02036   86–12300
ISBN: 0-8091-2811-X

Published by Paulist Press
997 Macarthur Boulevard
Mahwah, New Jersey 07430

Printed and bound in the
United States of America

Contents

To my Jesuit brothers
who have vividly shown me
by their examples
both how to say mass
and how not *to say mass!*

PRENOTES

1. For easy reference, I have included, wherever possible, references to *Documents of the Liturgy: 1963–1979* published by The Liturgical Press. These are indicated by the letters DOL followed by the paragraph number found in the book. This cross referencing has also been done by the excellent Canadian publication, the *National Bulletin on Liturgy*.

2. This book is *not* exclusively geared for priests. It is directed to *all* who have an active role in the liturgy of the Church, i.e., bishops, priests, deacons, readers, acolytes, musicians, liturgy committee members, active Christians. However, a stance had to be taken, and I decided to address my remarks primarily toward the presiders of the eucharist. Nevertheless, these remarks, in many cases, can also be taken to heart by many others, e.g. members of liturgy committees. In many situations, a committee may actually shape a given liturgy, and the presider merely follows a predetermined script, blindly (and sometimes inaccurately) believing that "the committee members must know what they are doing."

My major concern is to awaken people, particularly presiders of the eucharist, to the authentic celebration of the renewed eucharist in the Roman Rite. I have not attempted, as some have done elsewhere, to suggest ways to *adapt* the Roman Rite to a "better" form. Because of this particular concern, readers who are associated with "progressive" communities may find the remarks which follow obvious or even boring, and wonder why so much effort went into a project with so little applicability. However, my experience of liturgy has been different. The vast majority of presiders and Christians seem to be woefully ignorant about the basics of liturgy, as judged from the externals of the (by-the-book) liturgies that are celebrated, and so, the remarks which follow are directed primarily to help them. However, my experience has also been that *adapted* liturgies can be as un-liturgical as "by-the-book" liturgies, when presided over by individuals (and assisted by other ministers) who do not have a true sense of the symbolic nature of the renewed liturgy and an appropriate sense of drama as applied to liturgical ministry and movement. Re-writing prayers, re-arranging sections of the liturgy, re-assigning liturgical roles will not, *of themselves,* lead to a "better" liturgy, if the foundations of liturgy are ignored, that is, if the leaders of the liturgy ignore the basic symbols and fundamental gestures involved in the 2000 year tradition of Christian worship. My hope is that this book will awaken the reader to those fundamental concerns, no matter what his or her background is like.

Section 1

INTRODUCTION

In the "good old days" (although many would debate how "good" they actually were), we (thought we) knew what the Mass was about—it was the mystery of transubstantiation—it was the Sacrament of Communion. It "worked" *ex opere operato,* and since it was in Latin anyway, no one really had to worry about intelligibility or "style." *Symbol* was suspect—Protestants talked about Christ's "symbolic" presence in the eucharistic elements. But Catholics were concerned about "real" presence. Even though the *Baltimore Catechism* told us that "a sacrament is an outward sign, instituted by Christ, to give grace," not very many Catholics really took the meaning of "outward sign" too seriously. Sacraments were signs only insofar as they could be perceived by the senses. What was *really* important was the "matter" and "form" (as expounded in Aristotelean metaphysics, "baptized" by St. Thomas Aquinas, and defined by the Council of Florence in the 15th century)—the right "stuff" (like bread, wine, blessed oil, blessed water), and the correct words. As long as the right words were said with the right stuff (or over the right people), the sacrament "worked"—it "took"—it was "valid," i.e. it did not have to be repeated. Grace was guaranteed—since that is what *ex opere operato* was all about.

However, liturgical studies based on the decades-old "Liturgical Movement" have, at least on one level, changed all that. Even in official documents and books, we see an emphasis on sign, symbol, and style. Contemporary authors describe sacraments in ways that might scandalize our ancestors, yet in words which are probably closer to the original sense of what was happening, at least as far as the first few generations of Christians were concerned. For example, American theologian Tad Guzie writes:

> A sacrament is a festive action in which Christians assemble to celebrate their lived experience and to call to heart their common story. The action is a symbol of God's care for us in Christ. Enacting the symbol brings us closer to one another in the church and to the Lord who is there for us.[1]

Or take the definition of liturgy proposed by Father David Power:[2]

> The liturgy is an action wherein the testimony of God is heard and appropriated, the experience of the community is transformed, and a godly presence disclosed.

Even in official Roman documents, we see a dramatic shift in emphasis (sometimes inconsistently juxtaposed with older formulations) in the *Praenotanda* or *Introductory Remarks* to the revised liturgical rites. Take, for example, the comments on sign and symbol mentioned in the *General Instruction of the Roman Missal* (GIRM) concerning the bread to be used at mass (#283, DOL-1673) (emphasis added): "The *nature of the sign demands* that the material for the eucharistic celebration truly have the appearance of food."

And this excerpt is not a unique, isolated instance of this newer mindset, a mindset concerned with the authenticity of the signs used in liturgical celebrations. Perhaps a few other references would also be appropriate.

> *1981 Introduction to the Lectionary* (#35) Along with the ministers, the actions, the lectern, and other elements, the books containing the readings of the word of God remind the hearers of the presence of God speaking to his people. Since, in liturgical celebrations, the books too serve as *signs and symbols* of the sacred, care must be taken to ensure that they truly are worthy and beautiful.

> (GIRM #56h, DOL-1446h) It is most desirable that the faithful receive the Lord's body from hosts consecrated at the same

Mass and that, in the instances when it is permitted, they share in the chalice. Then *even through the signs* communion will stand out more clearly as a sharing in the sacrifice actually being celebrated.

(GIRM #240, DOL-1630) Holy communion has a more complete form *as a sign* when it is received under both kinds. For in this manner of reception a fuller light shines *on the sign* of the eucharistic banquet.

Pastoral Care of the Sick—1983 English language edition (#107) If the anointing is to be *an effective sacramental symbol,* there should be a generous use of oil so that it will be seen and felt by the sick person *as a sign* of the Spirit's healing and strengthening presence. For the same reason, it is not desirable to wipe off the oil after the anointing.

This re-sensitization to the role of symbol in liturgy needs to be taken to heart if we are really to bring the liturgy alive in our contemporary world. Even after more than 20 years since the promulgation of the Second Vatican Council's *Constitution on the Liturgy,* we have not come to grips with the implications and thrust of the renewed liturgy. As one commentator wrote, it is not that the new liturgy has been tried and found lacking, it is that it has never really been tried.

A major problem with the far past with regard to liturgy is that we had too many symbols, the majority of which had nothing really to do with what was important. The problem that exists in the recent past and the present is that we reacted too violently against that heritage, have thrown out *all* symbols, and have resorted to words to such an extent that our liturgies become an avalanche of words and still ignore the primary symbols. And this avalanche of words is, upon closer analysis, merely a re-working of the worst of an older liturgical theology.

The mis-use of symbols and signs is also related to a spirit of efficiency, convenience and minimalism that pervades the American way-of-life. McDonald's restaurants and IBM personal computers are becoming the paradigm for good liturgies and good liturgical practice. But people are not machines, and what may be tolerable as an occasional convenience in a busy world, can become significantly detrimental in the world of divine life and love.

Perhaps this idea is better expressed in the following quote from an issue of the Canadian *National Bulletin on Liturgy* (emphasis added):

> The Church uses symbols in celebrating the liturgy. It is *not the material element alone, but our use of it that is symbolic:* we use water in the baptismal bath, bread and wine in the eucharistic meal, oil in the anointing of the body in various rites. If *we use the symbol generously,* we are reflecting God's generous gifts to us in Christ. If we are miserly, using the minimum of gestures and actions, we prevent others from seeing and feeling the fullness of God's love. A Church that limits itself to *minimalism will be stunted in its faith and liturgy* and growth in love.[3]

Because our communal worship is centered on symbol, it cannot be overemphasized how important it is to use the important symbols well, and not let them be overwhelmed by what is relatively minor. This will lead to a better total celebration. There is still too much of the old mentality of "just so long as the right words are said, that is really all that is necessary." Too many of us learned the meaning of *ex opere operato* too well in the days before Vatican II, and even after over 20 years, we cannot put that into a secondary position. Recent clinical studies indicate that only about 20% of human communication is verbal—the other 80% is non-verbal. It is important to use symbol well, for that is the way that most of the communication is taking place during our celebrations. Unfortunately, we approach liturgy the same way we approach so many other things in our cerebral, technological world—with a rationalism that causes love to wane and the heart to wither. It is this approach which has worked against a better liturgy in our contemporary world. As Father David Power remarks,

> it is worth reflecting on [the contemporary symbol crises], in order to perceive the better what issues are at stake in the renewal of liturgy as a symbol system, and also perhaps to un-

derstand why too cerebral and organizational an approach to liturgical change has not borne the fruits apparently intended.[4]

The document *Environment and Art in Catholic Worship,* issued with the approval of the American bishops in 1978, devotes two paragraphs to the concept of "Opening Up of Symbols," and it is worthwhile to recall what this document says, particularly since it brings up the question of liturgical minimalism, and since it is an official liturgical document issued by a group of Church leaders.

14. Every word, gesture, movement, object, appointment must be real in the sense that it is our own. It must come from the deepest understanding of ourselves (not careless, phony, counterfeit, pretentious, exaggerated, etc.). Liturgy has suffered historically from a kind of minimalism and an overriding concern for efficiency, partly because sacramental causality and efficacy have been emphasized at the expense of sacramental signification. As our symbols tended in practice to shrivel up and petrify, they became much more manageable and efficient. They still 'caused,' were still 'efficacious' even though they had often ceased to signify in the richest, fullest sense.

15. Renewal requires the opening up of our symbols, especially the fundamental ones of bread and wine, water, oil, the laying on of hands, until we can experience all of them as authentic and appreciate their symbolic value.

The Canadian *Bulletin* also reminds us of the importance of the symbolic in our lives over and above the merely legal:

The quality of celebration has a strong effect on all who take part. Celebrations which are weak, slovenly, hasty, verbose, unprepared, or indifferent will weaken the faith of all present. Celebrations which are strong, joyful, carefully prepared, and well celebrated will help to deepen the faith and love of the participants. Good celebrations are a sign of our faith, and can strengthen it in all who share in the event.[5]

These same ideas were stated in slightly different words in another statement approved by the American bishops, entitled *Music in Catholic Worship:*

> 4. People in love make signs of love, not only to express their love but also to deepen it. Love never expressed dies. Christians' love for Christ and for one another and Christians' faith in Christ and in one another must be expressed *in the signs and symbols of celebration* or they will die.

> 6. Faith grows when it is well expressed in celebration. Good celebrations foster and nourish faith. Poor celebrations may weaken and destroy it.[6]

The criteria we use to determine whether a given celebration was "good" can no longer be reduced to merely checking whether the rubrics had been exactly followed. One reason for this is that the present rubrics do not exactly determine actions and options now as they did in the Tridentine Missal. Many times the rubrics specify multiple options. (For example, look at the following rubric from the Latin edition of the Rite of Anointing the Sick, #73: "The following litany may be said here, or after the anointing, or even, according to circumstances, at some other point. The priest may adapt or shorten the text." One would be hard pressed to find a more liberal rubric anywhere!) Other times, the rubrics give underlying principles and leave the exact execution to the sensibilities of the presider. (For example, in the Rite of Penance, we read in #41—"When the penitent comes to confess his sins, the priest welcomes him warmly and greets him with kindness.") Thus, in our contemporary world, our contemporary liturgies must be judged by contemporary standards based on contemporary insights into the nature of liturgy, of sacred symbol, and the human longing for divine love.

This book is an attempt to open eyes to some of the contemporary insights and contemporary standards. The attempt is by way of the *via negativa,* the method of counterexamples. It is a method which has been used for centuries both in theology and science, especially physics and mathematics. One learns about a concept through looking at what a concept should NOT be. We cannot really say much positive about God, for example. But we can affirm what God is NOT. It is hoped that the negative rules, examples, and principles given throughout this manuscript may give rise to positive results—to a positive appreciation of what the revised vision of the liturgy is really about, to a positive appreciation of what should be absent and present in good liturgy, to a positive appreciation of how Tridentine practices still creep into our liturgies to the detriment of the sacramental experience for post-Vatican II Christians.

But does this negative approach lead to a depressing outlook? Not necessarily. In fact, this negative-to-positive approach even has scriptural foundations. The majority of the Ten Commandments are phrased negatively—but they form the basis of a very positive covenant with God. In Luke's version of the Beatitudes (Lk 6:20–26), the four (positive) beatitudes are matched with four (negative) woes. Together, they describe a balanced pattern of life for a follower of the Lord. On the other hand, Christ's warning to the Pharisees was all negative in Matthew's gospel (23:13–36). Yet, this is interpreted as positive teaching for Christ's followers.

Some might accuse me of being "nitpicky," of making liturgical mountains out of rubrical molehills. It is true that all rubrics are *not* of equal importance. In the *Decree on Ecumenism* of the Second Vatican Council, we are told that "in Catholic doctrine, there exists an order or 'hierarchy' of truths" (ch. 2, #11), and the same principle also holds in liturgy—some things are more important than others. However, too often the impression is given at certain liturgies that everything is of equally little value. Details are important—attention to detail is what makes a good performance, whether it be a play, a symphony, or a dinner. Father Robert Hovda, formerly of The Liturgical Conference, writing about details and the liturgy,[7] quotes the words of William Blake which seem very apropos: "He who would do good to others must do it in minute particulars; 'General Good' is the plea of the scoundrel, hypocrite & flatterer. For art & science cannot exist but in minutely organised particulars, And not in generalizing demonstrations of the rational power." There are too many liturgies which are being evaluated as "generally good," but, upon closer examination (of the minute particulars), leave much to be desired. Like a good recipe, the minute details of the spices help bring out the flavor of the main entree—the spices should not drown out the main entree, but help us appreciate it. The same holds true for liturgy.

It may also seem that this book is overly-concerned with liturgical law and the many rubrics that exist, and not really concerned about the underlying spirit. In one sense, it is correct that rubrics are emphasized in the sections which follow, but only because I believe that law tries to enflesh more important underlying principles and less important cultural options for the purpose of preserving the heritage within a given tradition and in a cultural manner which most people would feel comfortable with. But law is only one aspect of what liturgy totally is—liturgy also involves culture, theology, psychology, history, to name a few other "supporting" disciplines. We can break a law and at the same time be on very good grounds theologically, psychologically, symbolically, historically and culturally. But, in my experience, that occurs rarely. More often, when rubrics are violated, other aspects of the liturgical experience are damaged as well, and this book is concerned with the total experience—an experience which should help lead people to a deeper love and praise of their God. In some situations, a law can be good—eliminating bad liturgical practices, like the law which states that there should be no music during the eucharistic prayer.[8] We do not need competition during the most important prayer of the mass. However, the same law can be enforced counter-liturgically, when an instrument is needed to help a presider sing the eucharistic prayer and the assembly sing their acclamations. In cases like these, we do well to respectfully "violate" an unliturgical interpretation of the law, without violating its fundamental purpose and spirit. My intent is to help the reader to learn the true spirit of what may seem to be very confusing (and at times anti-liturgical) rubrics and liturgical laws. We need always remember that just because something is legal does not make it morally right or personally expedient—take the legality of brothels in Nevada, or of abortions in the United States. Similarly, just because something is illegal does not make it morally evil—it is legal for the Byzantine Rite to use leavened bread at the eucharist, but not for the Roman Rite. Law is more complicated than we tend, at times, to admit. Law is also less absolute than we tend, at times, to practice.

Although the suggestions which follow are given as absolutes, very little is really absolute in this world. The wording is occasionally strong to indicate the importance which many liturgists attach to the topic under discussion, but some of the practices may allow for variation in special circumstances. However, when the *special* becomes the *typical,* then the general thrust of good liturgy may (quite possibly) be ignored, and then the liturgical experience of the assembly will suffer.

NOTES

(1) Guzie, *The Book of Sacramental Basics,* p. 53.

(2) Power, *Unsearchable Riches,* p. 146.

(3) Canadian *National Bulletin on Liturgy,* v. 16, #91 (Nov-Dec, 1983), p. 215.

(4) Power, *Unsearchable Riches,* p. 10.

(5) Canadian *Bulletin,* v. 16, #91 (Nov-Dec, 1983), p. 221.

(6) *Music in Catholic Worship,* First Edition 1972, Second Edition 1983.

(7) Hovda, "It Begins With The Assembly," in *A Reader: The Environment for Worship,* p. 41, quoting William Blake, "Jerusalem, Emanation of the Giant Albion," Ch. 3, plate 55, lines 60-63.

(8) cf. *Inaestimabile Donum,* #6; GIRM #12, DOL-1402 and footnote R1.

Section 2

SOME THOUGHTS ON SYMBOLS

Reverence symbols in all areas of life.

Symbols exist everywhere, but they reach a certain apex in our spiritual life in their presence in the eucharistic celebration. It is a highly symbolic gesture when a husband gives his wife a rose. But if the rose is given every year on their wedding anniversary, much more meaning is conveyed than the presence of a simple rose. So it is with the Eucharist—it makes more sense when we see it in context with the other symbols in our religious lives and see the religious symbols in context with symbols in non-religious aspects of our lives. As Father David Power says:

> Liturgy is not the sole symbolic reality, but it belongs alongside the scriptures and other manifestations such as icons. It is distinct from these not in being symbolic but in being the gathering and celebration of the body, the place where the church assumes its full form, bringing into a common expression of faith and joy all the other symbols that belong in this mystery.[1]

To re-iterate, sometimes we tend to overlook significant symbols in our lives, much to the detriment of inter-personal relationships. People of other cultures interpret gestures much more symbolically and can be offended because of our pragmatic attitude toward certain actions and things. Let me give you two significant examples which occurred a few years ago.

In November, 1979, Pope John Paul II traveled to Turkey, to Istanbul to meet with Orthodox Patriarch Dimitrios I. Gifts were exchanged—but most people overlooked the great symbolism attached to those gifts.[2] The Pope gave the Patriarch a replica of one of the most famous icons of the Roman Church, a copy of the icon of Our Lady of Czestochowa—this symbolized the Roman Church's devotion to the Mother-of-God, and her reverence of iconography, a "sacramental" in Orthodoxy. The Patriarch gave the Pope an Omophorion—the Byzantine equivalent of the Pallium, which is used by all Byzantine Rite bishops as a sign of their authority. This symbolized that Orthodoxy recognized the episcopacy and episcopal authority of the Pope, even though they do not agree with his universal jurisdiction. More than being mere trinkets, these two gifts were signs of willingness to acknowledge the truth of each Church's positions on significant issues.

After the Pope was shot, he left his recovery bed to briefly speak at a meeting between Orthodox and Catholics held in St. Peter's on Pentecost. He mentioned the writings of "St. Gregory Palamas," a theologian who died after the formal break between East and West in 1054. Gregory is held in high esteem among the Orthodox and his feast is celebrated on the Second Sunday of Lent. However, he has never been celebrated in the West and among Eastern Christians in union with Rome. Also he was never officially canonized by the Roman Church because of questionable theology. Nevertheless, the Pope referred to him as "Saint" Gregory, another extremely symbolic gesture which probably did more to heal the division between east and west than a whole series of theological discussions.

Symbols are extremely important in life—however, we too often overlook them or ignore them, because they are not as explicit and practical as we might want them to be. We need to be less practical and more reverential when we approach the symbols of liturgy.

Remember that the basic symbol of the Eucharist is one bread and one cup.

If we do not pay attention to the central elements of the eucharist, we are missing the boat. If the elements are obscured, something is wrong. If the fullness of the central symbols are withheld from the assembly (e.g., no communion from the cup), it is an impoverished liturgical experience.

One-ness is important, and newer legislation insists that only one vessel of bread and one cup should be used during the eucharistic prayer, until the breaking of the bread (see section 7). This symbolically emphasizes one of the "fruits" of the mass—the unity of the community.

The bread should look like bread, and even the Sacramentary demands this authenticity of sign (cf. GIRM #283, DOL-1673), but home-baked bread is not an absolute value over the fundamental sign of one bread and one cup. It is humorous to see home-baked little "hosts," or to see home-baked bread pre-cut into small sections before the liturgy begins. Granted it is necessary to have enough elements, and not over-consecrate, but one should not value this at the expense of a more basic symbol of the liturgy!

Do not do damage to strong liturgical symbols through unnecessary clutter.

One of the basic liturgical principles is to recognize the major symbols and enhance them. But enhancing in the liturgy frequently means permitting the symbols to stand on their own rather than drown them in clutter. Architecturally, the focal points of liturgy in a church are the altar (a symbol of Christ in the Book of Revelation), the font, the lectern, the chair. To make one piece of furniture compete with the others, or to clutter the furniture in such a way that one wonders what is what (e.g. to turn the altar into the cave of Bethlehem at Christmas) is far from being good liturgical practice.

Ideally, the altar initially should have *nothing* on it (including candles—they are better placed around the altar than on it). After the entrance procession, the Gospel Book, if used, should be the only item present on the altar. Then, after the procession with the gifts, ideally there should be only one cup and one loaf (cf. 1 Cor 10) on the altar—nothing more should be visible (the Sacramentary is tolerated, but among the Russian Byzantines, even the Sacramentary is not allowed on the altar!). (See section 7 for comments on what to do if more bread and wine are needed for the communion of the assembly.) To also put cruets and a finger bowl on the altar when movable credence tables can be discretely located nearby should be considered as a crime against good liturgy. To have the chalice on the altar from the beginning of the mass should be considered far less than ideal. A presider should not make the altar into the pastor's desk, similar to the presidential desk used for speeches to the nation. If you are the president, it may be appropriate to have microphones visible, along with pictures of the wife and kids, a pen and pencil set, reading glasses, speech notes, etc. on the desk top, but the altar is not a desk and it should be reserved for the symbols of Christ alone—one loaf, one cup, the book of the gospels (and, in contemporary society, to aid the memory of the presider, the Sacramentary—although this was not needed in the early church). Thus, a modern presider should take care to remove missalettes, reading glasses, homily notes, ugly microphones, etc. from the table of the Lord!

Do not distract from the praise of God with unexpected symbolic clashes!

Psalm 150 suggests that we praise God with "clashing cymbals," but more often than not, clashing *symbols* detract from the praise of God rather than adding to it.

I was startled by a conversation I had several years ago with a professor of communication who is fairly well-respected in his field. He told me how jarring it was for him to watch one of the televised masses of Pope John Paul II. The point of irritation was the fairly modern watch the Pope was wearing which was quite visible whenever close-ups of the Pope were shown.

My acquaintance, who over the years had become sensitive to subliminal forms of communication, body language, and the power of symbols, said that he was very struck by the Pope, as a symbol of the permanence of Christianity, celebrating the eucharist, a symbol of an eternal God's infinite love for the human race, with this blaring symbol of a modern, time-conscious culture. Instead of being drawn beyond the limits of this world, my friend felt himself being pulled into the worst aspects of the present speed-conscious culture.

This is just one example of symbolic clashes which can and do occur during the liturgy. Few, if any, help the community's prayer-life. Thus, we must constantly be sensitive to such possible clashes and eliminate them as much as possible.

Do not underestimate the subconscious power of symbols.

Robert Burns, in his poem, "To a Mouse," has given us words appropriate for many human situations:

> The best-laid schemes o' mice an' men
> Gang aft a-gley.

No matter how hard we plan, our schemes "gang aft a-gley," that is, often do go awry. One of the greatest planning disasters in recent history in the United States was the introduction of the Susan B. Anthony dollar coin. The reasons given for its introduction were, for the most part, well thought out and promising. However, the project was an abysmal failure. Many would attribute its failure to an unspoken, symbolic problem: "How can this coin be a dollar when it looks like a quarter? It's un-American to have a dollar that small! A dollar should be a paper bill or big enough to put into a Nevada slot machine."

On the rational, cerebral level, the Susan B. Anthony dollar was a money-saving answer to a great problem—the rapid wearing-out of paper dollar bills. But none of the planners realized the symbolic problems that it would raise and the possible failure of the plan due to these non-rational, non-practical, yet very real symbolic concerns.

I would suggest that we frequently do similar things in liturgies. Our cerebral plans may seem to "work," but on the symbolic level they are disasters, since they do not perdure nor do they increase the faith-commitment of members of the community. We too easily tend to dismiss the more important symbols of our liturgy—baptism by immersion, Communion under both kinds—as being impratical. But the Anthony dollar coin was meant to be practical and it still did not work! Practicality *can* be an enemy of good liturgy, if it overwhelms a fundamental symbol, disguises it, or reduces it to a bare minimum. We need to identify the basic symbols of our liturgy, enhance them (without worrying about efficiency or practicality), experience the fullness of these symbols, and only then plan about the secondary aspects of the rites. If we let our fundamental symbols speak for themselves to the fullest extent possible, we may learn that other parts of the liturgy are much easier to plan, and we may avoid "Susan B. Anthony"-type liturgical disasters.

NOTES

(1) Power, *Unsearchable Riches*, p. 47.
(2) cf. *Origins*, v. 9 (Nov 1979), p. 421.

Section 3

SOME THOUGHTS ON PRESIDERS

Presiders should preside.

Presiding is a developed art-form, akin to being a good orchestra conductor. Presiders need to know how to delegate, because being a presider differs from being a factotum. Presiders also need to know when and how to exercise leadership, yet allowing their leadership to reflect the awe of mystery of communicating with the Divine.

A number of presiders have a "stained-glass-window" voice which projects timidity rather than strength. Others seem to hide in the background in the name of "baptismal equality" and "democracy." One should not negate the theological truth that we are all equal (in one sense) through our common baptism, and that democracy has a role even in a hierarchical Church structure. Nevertheless, the liturgy needs leadership in the same way that an orchestra needs a conductor. Therefore, one of the continuing tasks of priests is to learn how to preside better, so that they might better serve the assembled People of God.

For a number of years recently, the Davies Symphony Hall in San Francisco has been sold out for the pre-Christmas "singalong" performances of Handel's *Messiah*. This is a beautiful "secular" parallel of what good liturgy and presiding should be about. The conductor (= presiding priest) is a must! The musicians (= ministers of word, music, eucharist) are also a must! The audience (= assembly) is also a must if this is to be the experience that everyone present hopes it will be. The conductor (= presiding priest) does not do everything by himself, but his services are necessary. Unfortunately for the parallel, the orchestra conductor usually doesn't sing or play the major solo as a presiding priest must do during the liturgy (i.e., the eucharistic prayer), but this parallel does bring out how a good liturgy is a coordination of efforts.

Do not underplay the role of the Presider.

Father Robert Hovda suggests that the presider has five major tasks to perform in the liturgy.[1]

(1) *Directing the entire service* while leaving to other ministers other roles. The presider must graciously coordinate ministries while still remaining "in charge" of the entire worship service.

(2) *Defining the beginning and end of the entire service.*

(3) *Leading prayer, in particular the eucharistic prayer.* In the Roman tradition, the presider formulates and voices five prayers in the course of the liturgy—the Opening Prayer, the Prayer concluding the General Intercessions, the Prayer over the Gifts, the Eucharistic Prayer, and the Prayer after Communion. The eucharistic prayer is, of course, the high point of the presider's praying, but not the only one he does. Note that this also demands that other prayers (such as the Prayer concluding the General Intercessions) not be sub-delegated to others either.

(4) *Distributing communion with his own hand.* A point made by Father Godfrey Diekmann, O.S.B. in his research into historical texts is that a key role of the presider is to distribute communion from the elements that he consecrated, an action which is intimately connected with proclaiming the eucharistic prayer. Therefore one must question the practice of letting others do the work of distributing communion on the (shaky) basis that "all the priest has to do is say the words of consecration." One also has to question the practice frequently seen when bishops celebrate—of letting the priests distribute communion, while the bishop rests at the chair.

(5) *Proclaiming the word.* This is a normal task for the presider, although it may happen that it can be delegated to another, for example a concelebrant or a deacon. (However, as will be

noted in section 6, "proclaiming the word" does *not* mean that the presider must himself read the scripture during the liturgy.)

Do not overplay the role of the Presider.

A re-occuring theme in various documents is that "all, whether minister or laypersons, should do all and only those parts [of the liturgy] that belong to them."[2] A presider should not usurp the functions of the other ministers, nor should he over-delegate presidential functions to them. In planning the liturgy, he needs to solicit advice from his co-workers, yet, since he is ultimately the sole presider, he should not let others make all decisions pertaining to his role.

The presider should never look like a reluctant sorcerer dragged in to say the magic words at the right time while others are "really" running the "show." Liturgy, like an orchestral performance, is a coordination of efforts, prayers, talents and deferences so that the end result is that God is praised, rather than the ministers receiving pats on their backs.

Do not forget about the congregation.

The liturgy is not something the presiding-priest does FOR the people, it is something the assembled group of Christians, whose gifts are coordinated by a presider, does TOGETHER. *Environment and Art* reminds us of this truth:

> Among the symbols with which liturgy deals, none is more important than this assembly of believers. . . . The most powerful experience of the sacred is found in the celebration and the persons celebrating, that is, it is found in the action of the assembly: the living words, the living gestures, the living sacrifice, the living meal. This was at the heart of the earliest liturgies.[3]

Never merely "say mass"!

Gone are the days when all a priest had to do was "say mass." However, the mentality lingers and negatively infects many a eucharistic gathering. The presider must exercise a position of loving, serving leadership in the assembly of the baptized, but he can never totally substitute for the assembly and should never usurp ministries which properly belong to others. Therefore, it is wrong for a presider to always proclaim all the readings himself, if there are competent readers in the assembly. It is wrong for a presider to ignore the legitimate demands of the assembly. It is wrong for a presider to preside as if the assembly were merely frosting on the cake, and not the meat of the meal.

Do not usurp another's proper part.

More than one presider has the bad habit of saying "Amen" when he should not do so, for example as the conclusion to the initial sign of the cross. By doing this, he is usurping a response which properly belongs to the assembly, and depriving them of active participation in the liturgical action at that point. This can have detrimental effects in other places. If enough presiders do this sort of thing often enough, one has the reverse of the Pavlov's dog syndrome—instead of always responding when given the cue, the assembly is lulled into non-response.

Do not forget that a Presider is a public figure in a quasi-dramatic setting.

Because the presider is a public figure, things that might perhaps be tolerable in private become rude and offensive in the liturgical context. Because the liturgy is, in effect, a quasi-dramatic setting using stylized movements, "choreography," and a "script," many of the common-sense guidelines for actors are also applicable to all the ministers of the liturgy.

For example, all ministers should vest with care. Dangling ends of cinctures should never be permitted.

When speaking to the assembly, ministers should keep proper eye contact with the assembly. Few things are as counter-symbolic as a presider who is looking at the book while saying, "The Lord be with you"!

When speaking to the people, ministers should make sure they are heard, gently ignoring, if need be, the microphone system. Too often, ministers assume that since there is a microphone in front of them, they do not have to project, or they can even tone down their voice to merely a whisper. In many situations, this can be disastrous. Most P.A. systems are set so that only a normal speaking voice is amplified properly, and frequently church P.A. systems leave a lot to be desired. As a result, in some churches, a presider might fight against the electronic "helps" to make himself heard by the assembly!

Do not do damage to the shape and flow of the liturgy.

Many presiders preside as if the liturgy were a disparate juxtaposition of non-related rites. Most scholars would agree that the various parts of the liturgy are all inter-connected, but it requires special concentration for a presider to convey this to the assembly. Too often, some presiders seem to not be aware of the flow of the liturgy and even seem to be building dams to stop the flow at various points. Such presiders need to be encouraged to take time to re-acquaint themselves with the liturgy, its unity, its various parts, and their interconnections.

Do not make gestures as if you were a robot.

The gestures of the liturgy are human gestures, even though they are somewhat stylized, dramatic gestures. The mentality of the pre-Vatican II liturgy forced presiders to perform the major gestures as if the presiders were robots performing strange magical rites, and unfortunately, many a presider whose formation took place before 1965 still clings to this style (albeit perhaps unconsciously).

There are four major hand/arm gestures which should be commented on, to clarify both how they are done, and when they are done.

JOINED HANDS are used when a presider talks to the assembly, e.g. when saying "let us pray," before the opening prayer, or when introducing the General Intercessions.

EXTENDED ("Greeting") HANDS are used when GREETING the assembly, e.g., when saying "The Lord be with you." This should be seen as a human gesture imitating the gesture one would make right before embracing a friend.

EXTENDED ("Praying") HANDS are used for presidential public prayers. This gesture is NOT used for private prayers (e.g., the prayers before communion), and it is also NOT used for introductions to prayers which are addressed to the assembly (e.g. "Let us pray"). This should also be seen as a human gesture of reaching out to heaven, with palms almost straight up, hands about head high, arms about half-way between being straight out from the side and straight ahead.

EXTENDED ("Imposition") HANDS are used in blessings and gestures of sanctification. This is a stylized variant of the human gesture of a gentle touch. It is used especially at ordination, but also in reconciling sinners, in anointing the sick, and at confirmation. During the eucharist, this is the gesture made over the gifts during the epicletic section of the eucharistic prayer, and also over the assembly during a solemn blessing or prayer over the people.

Beware of omitting gesture.

Among the standard equipment that every religious sister possessed when teaching grammar school was the clicker—that little device which resembled flat castanets, and which was used primarily to make a distinct sound. This sound was the key to when to stand or kneel or genuflect when in church.

Many of us have reacted to this regimentation, and especially in small group masses, have decided that "enlightened" Catholics have grown beyond gesture (and body posture).

However we are body-people. We communicate bodily, not via ESP. In the secular world we follow certain conventions, like standing when giving "standing ovations," or when dignitaries enter rooms. The Church has used these human conventions for centuries for the same basic reasons—they enable us bodily to express our belief in the importance of things or persons (standing or genuflecting), or to express unity (sitting or standing), or to express feelings (striking the breast or kneeling).

Gestures are important both for the assembly and for the presider. *Environment and Art* reminds us:

> The liturgy of the Church has been rich in a tradition of ritual movement and gestures. These actions, subtly, yet really, contribute to an environment which can foster prayer or which can distract from prayer. When the gestures are done in common, they contribute to the unity of the worshiping assembly. Gestures which are broad and full in both a visual and tactile sense, support the entire symbolic ritual. When the gestures are done by the presiding minister, they can either engage the entire assembly and bring them into an even greater unity, or if done poorly, they can isolate.[4]

We must not lightly dispense with posture changes, for example. It may be awkward in a small liturgy to stand for the gospel or to stand for the eucharistic prayer, but perhaps the awkwardness will just emphasize the importance of the given parts even more. It may seem like a minor thing to omit the sign of the cross at the beginning of the liturgy, or the crosses before the gospel, or kissing the gospel book, but these gestures help engage each Christian present, and re-iterate the truth that we do not worship God with our minds alone, but with "all our heart, all our soul, and all our strength" (Deut. 6:5).

Do not sing unless you can!

One should not abandon all hope of singing if one is not a Caruso or a Pavarotti, but one of the greatest crosses in the pre-

Vatican II Church was having to endure the cacaphonous warblings of an aging pastor who could not carry a tune in a bucket. Since nothing is absolutely required to be sung by a presider in the present Sacramentary, the presider need not worry about his inability to sing. Thus, a presider need not inflict his lack of talent on an assembly. On the other hand, singing can greatly enhance a liturgy if done with a certain minimal amount of competence. If a presider with at least a somewhat ordinary voice sings at least the preface and doxology of the eucharistic prayer, this can be a great encouragement to many in the assembly, also possessing ordinary voices, to sing their praise of God as well, and thus lead to a better overall liturgical experience for all present.

Do not neglect to prepare the physical implements.

In particular, prepare the Sacramentary. Do not flip through the pages of the Sacramentary while the assembly is responding. This is rude, impolite, and might even be considered a sin against good liturgy.

Never perform two (visible) actions at the same time.

This can be one of the natural results of not preparing well. Some presiders must find the opening prayer in the Sacramentary while the assembly is praying the Gloria. Others are counting out hosts into the plate while the assembly is proclaiming the Creed. If this type of behavior were done by actors in a play, the play would not last past opening night!

NOTES

(1) Hovda, *Strong, Loving and Wise,* pp. 36, 40.
(2) GIRM #58, DOL-1448; Constitution on the Liturgy, #28, DOL-28.
(3) *Environment and Art,* ##28-29.
(4) *Environment and Art,* #56.

Section 4

SOME GENERAL LITURGICAL PRINCIPLES

Do not take liturgical law too seriously nor too lightly.

The rubrics and other laws which describe and govern liturgy are *human* laws, and for the most part, can be modified in years ahead. Yet, they are an attempt to describe patterns of human behavior in a given formal situation (e.g. a eucharistic liturgy) based on tradition, theology, culture, the nature of symbol, the demands of the gospel, and the needs of the community.

As mentioned at the end of section 1, a given liturgical law can sometimes eliminate a bad liturgical practice, but in other situations, can be invoked in such a way as to stifle the development of good liturgy. The *law must be respected* because it offers us the wisdom of the ages and a method of incarnating liturgical principles into human actions. But the law is not an end in itself—only God's holy people, united by the Spirit in praising the Father of Jesus are such an end.

Never be comfortable with "shoddy worship."

The biblical story of Cain and Abel can be interpreted as a story about authentic versus shoddy worship. Abel presented the best to God—thus his sacrifice of praise was accepted. Cain was comfortable with second best—his sacrifice was not. How often in our eucharistic gatherings are we comfortable with second best, or even worse?

Do not make too much/little out of the mass.

The *Constitution on the Liturgy* tells us: "The liturgy is the summit toward which the activity of the Church is directed; at the same time it is the fountain from which all her power flows."[1] Yet, we are also told: "The sacred liturgy does not exhaust the entire activity of the Church. Before individuals can come to the liturgy they must be called to faith and to conversion."[2] And "the liturgy" is NOT synonymous with "the eucharist." The eucharistic liturgy is the summit of the entire liturgical life, and the liturgy (in general) is the summit of all Church activity. However, Church activity should not be identified with the eucharist alone. Yet, in the Roman Catholic tradition, there is a bad habit of being "over-eucharistized" to the detriment of other prayer forms. Home masses have been conducted at the drop of a hat, and for relatively insignificant reasons. The eucharist as summit of the liturgy makes sense only if there exist other forms of liturgy. And the liturgy as summit of the Church's activity makes sense only if there exist other forms of Church activity.

Do not substitute/emphasize minor parts/actions in lieu of major ones.

Father Robert Hovda gives a very good example of this type of problem:

> If, for example, in planning a eucharistic celebration, a group brings in a combo of musicians for song support, a batch of slides to help create an environment, a troupe of mime or dance specialists to illustrate the reading of the gospel, and does nothing about the bread and wine, it would not be unreasonable to send them all to bed without their suppers. . . . But, because we are accustomed to a symbolic minimalism with respect to all sacraments, we tend to think that we have to bring in all sorts of entirely new elements to save this wretched rite. . . . If we attended to the bread and wine, we would discover that the
> · rite is powerful indeed.[3]

Even so-called "liturgical" helps can be relatively un-liturgical. Hovda also writes: "A booklet on the celebration of baptism came to this author's desk a few years ago: it was full of suggestions about peripheral aspects of the celebration; it said nothing at all about the actual bathing, the washing with water."[4]

In *Music in Catholic Worship,*[5] we find a good evaluation of which parts of the eucharistic liturgical rite are primary and which are secondary. When secondary rites overshadow what is primary, we are left with bad liturgy. For example, the second half of the eucharist is shaped by the four verbs mentioned again and again in the New Testament at Last Supper accounts, at the multiplications of the loaves and fishes, and in the Emmaus account—taking, blessing, breaking and sharing. If a presider performs the actions of the mass so that the breaking of the bread is overshadowed by the kiss of peace or by the commingling of the bread and the wine, or the taking of the bread and wine is overshadowed by the washing of hands, or the breaking of the bread is telescoped into the prayer of blessing, the result is an impoverished liturgical experience for all present.

Do not mis-understand the positive qualities of the Roman liturgical tradition!

Edmund Bishop writes: "The genius of the native Roman Rite is marked by simplicity, practicality, a great sobriety and self-control, gravity and dignity . . . in two or three words . . . soberness and sense."[6] However, *practicality* does not necessarily mean *efficiency* as practiced by the secular American culture of the 1980's. And, the Roman Rite's concern for *simplicity* does not justify ignoring liturgical principles based on solid symbolic values. Too often, *liturgical* decisions nowadays are based on non-liturgical reasons in the name of so-called "simplicity and practicality," with the end result being a poor liturgy.

A simple example of mis-guided practicality would be the decision as to where the presider stands at various points of the liturgy. The Sacramentary directs three possible places at SPECIFIC TIMES—the chair for the opening and closing rites,[7] AND ALSO THE

LITURGY OF THE WORD (the presider needs to go to the lectern only if there is no deacon or assisting priest to read the gospel),[8] and the altar for the liturgy of the eucharist. Yet how often does one see a presider at the altar or the lectern for the opening rites, merely because it is too difficult to have an additional microphone at the chair. Here is a situation in which we have, in the name of simplicity and practicality, adapted the liturgy in a non-liturgical fashion.

As another example, take the decision as to the form and shape of the eucharistic bread. Certainly the typical form and shape of the communion breads or "hosts" as commonly found in most parishes are simple and practical, but here the simplicity and practicality is derived from a sense of efficiency that is alien to a fundamental symbol for the eucharist—the symbol found in scripture itself—the symbol of breaking one bread (cf. Luke 24, Acts 2, 1 Cor 10). Once again, we are basing liturgical judgments on non-liturgical concerns, much to the detriment of our worship experience.

Do not thematize what is fundamentally theme-less.

We do need to focus our energies and not let our liturgies float off to never-never land. But focusing frequently degenerates into "what is the theme of this liturgy?" The liturgy, ANY liturgy, has only one "theme"—giving thanks to God for his action in our world as particularly expressed through Christ's death and resurrection. Anything more is frosting on the cake. When we baptize, we incorporate someone into the body of Christ and therefore into Christ's death and resurrection. When we forgive, we do so by reason of the reconciliation won by Christ's death and resurrection. And so on with the rest of the liturgical rites.

However, frequently planning groups so struggle to find the "theme" and to make everything match, that damage is done to the liturgical experience.

Father Hovda writes:

> Properly understood, the theme is a modest attempt to capture
> in a few sentences a message in the readings in the context

both of the year and of the local human situation. However, the theme gets out of hand more frequently than one would wish. . . . Blessing God with thanks and praise is the fundamental and sufficient theme for any liturgical celebration.[9]

Benedictine Father Patrick Regan comments as follows:

Preoccupation with theme is as foreign to liturgy as it is to celebration in general. Celebration stems from events, not abstract concepts. Of course, thematic services do make use of evangelical events, but only insofar as they bear upon the chosen theme. By subordinating the gospel event to a previously agreed upon theme, the participants do not surrender to the event on its own terms, but grasp only that aspect of it which pertains to their purpose, thereby closing themselves to the possibility of receiving the event as it reveals and confers itself in its own freedom, and receiving instead more confirmation of their own thematic construct. This is neither celebration nor liturgy. It is self-gratification.[10]

Often a "theme" is provided by the feast or strong season being celebrated at the liturgy. For example, Christmas is about the birth of our Savior—that is "theme" enough—one need not examine the (four different sets of) readings to find another "theme." Similarly, Lent provides us with a time of preparation for re-celebrating the Paschal events of the death and resurrection of Christ, and for preparing catechumens for their baptism. In this general context, the various Sundays of Lent offer specific ways in which our thoughts can be renewed as we attempt to re-create our lives in Christ by remembering the sacred moments of his death and resurrection.

In this way, "theme" provides the ambience, the atmosphere (like a good restaurant) for "enjoying" the (sacred) meal. But it does not so dominate the celebration as to put the assembly, the presider, and the Spirit of God into a liturgical straight-jacket from which they cannot break forward into greater freedom before each other, and before God our Father.

I think many liturgies would be improved if people thought not so much in terms of "themes" which is passive and abstract, but rather in terms of "thrusts," "events," "challenges"—concepts which are more active and concrete.

Never turn the exceptional into the ordinary.

Liturgical practices should be based on an ideal, not a minimal. Certainly it is licit to administer baptism by pouring only a few drops of water over a child's forehead, but liturgical practice should be based on something which is symbolically more authentic, and the ideal for baptism is immersion (even if it cannot be done in every instance)! Similarly, it may be tolerated to have communion under one kind in large gatherings (e.g. a few thousand people), but arguing for communion under one kind in a small group simply to save a few minutes does not seem to be in the spirit of the new liturgy.

When adapting the liturgy, do not regularly omit certain options.

This is basically the same sage advice found in the Directory for Masses with Children (#40, DOL-2173). It suggests that, for example, the entrance rite should be adapted for masses with children, but that the various items which are omitted should be rotated, so that no one item is always omitted. This is wise advice for all liturgies, adapted or not. Some parishes and presiders NEVER use the option of blessing water for sprinkling in lieu of the penitential rite, for example. Some presiders always use option 1 or option 3 for the penitential rite. Some presiders always omit the washing of hands. These may not be wise moves, both for continuity with the universal church, and for a varied liturgy.

Avoid the "fireman" approach to liturgy.

In the pre-Vatican II era, it was a very common practice to have all the clergy at a parish on "fireman" duty all Sunday morning. One priest said mass, and at the right moment, another cleric would rush into the sanctuary to give the sermon. When that was done, the preacher left for another cup of coffee (unless he had to say a later mass) only to return (with the rest of the parish "troops") to distribute communion and then magically disappear again. Like firemen at a fire, they appeared from nowhere when needed, and then disappeared when the "emergency" was over.

The present Sacramentary is based on a renewed spirit of liturgical authenticity. Priests should not dress like deacons ever.[11] Super-monsignors should not dress like bishops.[12] Bread should look like food.[13] Communion should be distributed under both kinds when possible.[14] In this modern ambience, to have someone *not* a part of the total liturgical experience (i.e. not present *throughout* the liturgy) exercise a significant liturgical ministry (e.g. homilist or minister of communion) is compromising the authenticity of the symbol, and therefore leading to a poorer overall liturgy.

Certainly, there are circumstances that arise and even regularly exist in which the "fireman" approach must be tolerated. But while tolerating this less-than-ideal situation, those in charge should attempt to consider alternatives to virtually elminate the various practices (e.g. presiders homilizing, increasing the number of special communion ministers).

Do not ignore the presidential chair.

The presidential chair is a focal point of the liturgical action. It (and the lectern) are used even in those rites when the eucharist is not celebrated, e.g. the liturgy of the hours. It is symbolic of the need we have in human societies of someone to "chair" the meeting, or of the custom in most families of referring to "daddy's special chair." Liturgically, the presidential chair plays the same role in the typical church that the *cathedra* or bishop's chair plays in the diocesan Cathedral—it is symbolic of leadership for the community. It is NOT MERELY A CONCESSION TO HUMAN WEAKNESS, but rather a symbol.[15] In Byzantine Churches, a special chair is reserved for the bishop, even though he might use it only once every few years. Father Hovda reminds us that the chair is *not disposable*.[16] However, it is a place which should help the presider preside over the assembly both with strength and with concern, and, thus, the chair should not be a throne. When there are concelebrants, they should realize that presiding is a function of one person, not a committee, and there must be only ONE PRESIDENTIAL CHAIR—the sanctuary should not be re-arranged so that it looks as though the board of trustees of the school are jointly presiding over a graduation, or the board of directors of a corporation are jointly presiding over a meeting of stockholders. Concelebrants should be discretely seated on the side—for they are more a part of the assembly than appendages to the principal celebrant.[17]

Father Eugene Walsh, SS, offers these thoughts:

> The principle that determines, before all else, the best place for the presiding celebrant is what provides his immediate 'presence' to the celebrating community. . . . Nothing should interfere with the immediacy of his contact with the community. . . . The presiding celebrant does not need a throne . . . [but he] should have an attractive chair. . . . [F]or the strongest sign of leadership, the presiding celebrant should be seated alone.[18]

Never put a small cross on the altar.

The Tridentine missal prescribed that the presider had to look at the corpus on the altar cross at specific times (e.g. during the "offertory prayers"). This is no longer required, and in fact, the Sacramentary specifically requires that the major cross be visible to the assembly (GIRM #270, DOL-1660). Major signs are not duplicated in the new liturgy (GIRM #278, DOL-1668), hence there should not be a second cross on the altar solely for the benefit of the presider.

Never omit silence.

Most presiders do include a period of silence after communion, before the Prayer after Communion, but often this "silence" is "broken" by the purification of the sacred vessels. True silence is a silence for the entire assembly only when *everyone* is silently praying and no one, not even the presider, is doing anything. Moreover, only relatively few presiders take advantage of other places for silence, for example, after the invitation, "let us pray" before the Opening Prayer, after each of the readings, after the homily. These should also be true moments of silence, and not merely cursory nods in that direction.

NOTES

(1) Constitution on the Liturgy, #10, DOL-10.

(2) Constitution on the Liturgy, #9, DOL-9.

(3) cf. Hovda, *Strong, Loving and Wise*, p. 30.

(4) cf. Hovda, *Strong, Loving and Wise*, p. 30.

(5) *Music in Catholic Worship*, ##42–49.

(6) cf. Bishop, "The Genius of the Roman Rite," in *Liturgica Historica*, London and Toronto: OUP, 1918, 1962, pp. 12, 19. Quoted in the Canadian *Bulletin*, v. 11, #62 (Jan-Feb, 1978), p. 46; v. 17, #95 (Sept-Oct, 1984), p. 196, note 2.

(7) cf. GIRM #86, DOL-1476; GIRM #138, DOL-1528.

(8) cf. GIRM #97, DOL-1487; GIRM #99, DOL-1489.

(9) Hovda, *Strong, Loving and Wise*, p. 28.

(10) Regan, "Liturgy and the Experience of Celebration," p. 600.

(11) cf. Introduction to the 1972 changes in the GIRM, DOL-1372.

(12) cf. *Pontificalia Insignia*, #6, DOL-4454.

(13) GIRM #283, DOL-1673.

(14) GIRM #240-1, DOL-1630-1; cf. *This Holy and Living Sacrifice*, #19.

(15) cf. Emminghaus, *The Eucharist*, pp. 111–112.
(16) cf. Hovda, *Strong, Loving and Wise*, p. 54.
(17) cf. *Environment and Art*, #70.
(18) Walsh, *Practical Suggestions for Celebrating Sunday Mass*, pp. 18–19.

Section 5

THE ENTRANCE RITE

Do not bow to the cross instead of the altar.

The Tridentine Missal prescribed a bow to the altar, before
the presider opened the Missal and then started the prayers at the
foot of the altar, but this rubric was worded in a very interesting
way. It mentioned the reverence to the "altar, i.e. the image of the
Crucified One placed above it" ("et Altari, seu imagini Crucifixi
desuper positae, profunde se inclinat").[1] This suggests that the
reverence was primarily to the cross, and NOT to the altar. The
present Sacramentary (GIRM #84, DOL-1474) simply prescribes
a bow to the altar *without* any mention of the altar cross. Since
the "altar cross" may actually be the processional cross, it would
be very awkward for the presider to have to orient himself toward
the acolyte holding the cross to bow.

If the Blessed Sacrament is reserved somewhere in the sanctuary, a genuflection should be made toward It, but the bow toward the altar should not therefore be omitted. One should not
over-reverence the Reserved Sacrament during a ceremony
whose culmination is the Sacrament which is reserved! (In fact,
the 1984 *Ceremonial of Bishops* prescribes in #49 that if a bishop
celebrates at an altar at which the Sacrament is normally reserved
in a tabernacle, the Sacrament is to be *removed* during the liturgy.) Beware that presiders also "mis-orient" themselves during
prayer at other times, e.g. bowing toward the tabernacle instead
of the altar before the gospel (see section 6 below).

Avoid reciting the "introit."

The Foreword to the American edition of the Sacramentary makes this statement:

> Since these [Introit] antiphons [for the Entrance Rite] are too abrupt for communal recitation, it is preferable when there is no singing that the priest (or the deacon, other minister, or commentator) adapt the antiphon and incorporate it in the presentation of the Mass of the day. . . . The adaptation of the text of the entrance antiphon for this purpose is suggested by the Congregation for Divine Worship.

The implications of this statement are clear—the presider should *not* ask the congregation to "join me in reciting the introit on page 42 of your missalette." It is LESS THAN IDEAL for the presider to merely recite it himself. It is much better to use the scriptural phrase, patristic text, or ancient liturgical refrain given in the Sacramentary for "The Entrance Rite" as a springboard to introduce the feast or celebration and lead into the penitential rite.

Do not omit the sign of the cross.

The sign of the cross is word and gesture/action, and thus bears the qualities of a minor sacrament or "sacramental." It is body worship in addition to being mind worship. It recalls the significant gestures made in other sacramental rites—baptism, absolution, confirmation, anointing, blessings. To omit this action (unless the rubrics substitute another action for it, for example the reception of the casket in the Mass for Christian Burial) is to deprive the assembly of bodily worship, and also to deprive them of the possibility of recalling with St. Paul, that as Christians, "it behooves us to glory in the cross of our Lord Jesus Christ" (Gal. 6:14).

When making the sign of the cross, do not say "Amen."

Most of us have been at a Mass in which the presider began
the liturgy with a strange gesture, as if he were chasing flies away
from his face and trying to catch one in front of his chest, and an
even stranger statement (usually given in one breath), something
like: "In t'nay mov t'fath'r, so, nan holy spir ta men t'lord be wi
tyu." Avoid duplicating this at all costs!

The "Amen" is the response of the people and NOT of the presider, and in the Judeo-Christian liturgical tradition this word in
particular is a unique way of allowing individuals to affirm statements made by others. Hence, the importance of the "Amen" in
the worship services among black American Baptists, especially
during the sermons. By usurping this response, or making the
sign of the cross in such a way that the assembly is unable to respond properly, the entire worship-dialogue between presider and
assembly is off to a bad start. The assembly has been told (non-
verbally) that the presider does not want them to become involved—that he can do it all by himself. This may be the farthest
thing from a given presider's mind when he absent-mindedly says
"Amen" to the sign of the cross, but it sets up a psychological environment which is not well-suited to good worship.

Do not vary the initial greeting to lose its biblical origin.

The three sample greetings in the Sacramentary all have biblical origins. However, other greetings may be used in lieu of
these greetings, as a comparison with other liturgical rites issued
after the Sacramentary indicates[2] and as an examination of texts
used for papal liturgies indicates (usually a special "greeting" is
printed, along with the other prayer texts).[3] However, in these
cases, care is taken to model the new greeting on those found in
scripture.

Do not replace the "sacred greeting" with a "secular greeting."

American liturgist Ralph Keifer makes the following comments about the initial greeting:

> Distortion of the formal greeting ("Good morning," "The Lord *is* with you") is inappropriate—a violation of the ritual bond already established by the song and procession. To say something like "Good morning" is to say loud and clear that the ritual is a barrier to communication. It is felt as a break from pattern and is experienced as the celebrant's peeping over or around a wall of ritual at the people. . . . To say either "Good morning" or to change the greeting formula into a flat statement is to treat the congregation as if they were bored or ignorant.[4]

Benedictine Father Aidan Kavanagh essentially says the same thing:

> The reason for which some presidents choose to greet the assembly with "Good morning, everybody" instead of "The Lord be with you" is difficult to fathom. It cannot be that the former is more appropriate to the assembly's purpose than the latter. Nor can it be that the first is theologically more sophisticated than the second. And since one would prefer not to entertain the possibility that the secular greeting is a mark of clerical condescension to the simple and untutored laity, the only alternative is to attribute the secular greeting's use to presidential thoughtlessness of a fairly low order.[5]

These are both somewhat strong positions, perhaps too strong for each and every situation, but they make the point that some seemingly insignificant adaptations are not all that insignificant, if one takes a wider picture into view. Monsignor Joseph Champlin, another well-known American liturgist, takes a slightly milder approach, however.[6] He suggests that the presider might offer a simple "good morning" to the assembly in addition to the formal biblical greeting. He does grant that this somewhat duplicates the ritual greeting, and other liturgists suggest that the entrance rite already has four or five beginnings. Thus, an additional greeting does not seem to be in the interests of better liturgy.

When using the third penitential rite, (1) do not speak to the Father, the Spirit, or anyone other than Christ, and (2) do not dwell on human failures, but rather proclaim Christ's mercy and saving qualities.

Many older commentaries on the Tridentine Missal incorrectly stated that the triple *Kyrie* was addressed to each person of the Trinity, and in fact, the medieval tropes which embellished the sung *Kyries* in fact did include invocations to the Father and the Spirit. However, contemporary studies have shown that this text, borrowed from Eastern liturgies, was always intended to be addressed to Christ, and him alone. In most early texts, *Kyrie* (= Lord) is associated with the hymn in Philippians 2, where it is proclaimed that "Jesus Christ is LORD to the glory of God the Father." Thus, in the official examples for options for the third penitential rite given in the Sacramentary, it is always Christ who is addressed, never the Father or the Spirit (or Mary, or one of the Saints).[7]

In addition, the format of this version of the penitential rite should concentrate on divine mercy rather than human faults. In practice, this means that the "invocations" should NEVER INCLUDE THE WORD "WE" although they might occasionally tolerate the word "US" or "OUR." For example, it is INCORRECT to say:

> Lord, for the times WE have ignored our sisters and brothers,
> and looked at our own needs: Lord, have mercy.

Invocations of this style stress human failures to an undue degree for this part of the liturgy. That emphasis would be more appropriate for a litany of penitence during a Communal Penance Service, but not as a typical proclamation of praise of God's mercy.

Rather, the Sacramentary always focuses on Christ, and any

innovative invocations for this penitential rite should do likewise. For example,

Lord Jesus, Son of God: Lord, have mercy.
Lord Jesus, you are the Way: Lord, have mercy.
Lord Jesus, you heal our sins: Lord, have mercy.

Do not introduce a sign of the cross at the end of the penitential rite.

In the Tridentine Missal, the *Confiteor* ended with two declaratory formulae: "May almighty God have mercy on you . . . ," followed by "May the almighty and merciful Lord grant us pardon, absolution, and remission of all our sins." It was this *second*, quasi-absolution formula which was accompanied by a sign of the cross. However, in the present Sacramentary, this second formula has been omitted and the sign of the cross has *not* been transferred to the other formula.

Re-introducing a sign of the cross into the penitential rite is ill-advised as well as being contrary to the rubrics. This practice heightens the penitential rite, making it even more quasi-sacramental. However, most liturgists would like to downplay an independent penitential rite (and omit it whenever possible). The more authentic liturgical tradition is that minor sins are forgiven by open-heartedly hearing the Word of God and partaking in the eucharistic banquet. Emphasizing the penitential rite is like emphasizing hors d'oeuvres while overlooking that the primary nourishment (reconciliation) comes later.

Never modify the prayer endings so that the assembly will not be able to respond with their "Amen."

It seems such a minor adaptation to change "for ever and ever" to "for ever" or "forevermore," or to change "through Christ our Lord" to "through Jesus our Lord and Brother." And, basically, these truly are relatively minor adaptations. Yet, in terms of ritual action, of stimulus and response, of expectations, and of repetitions, such minor changes can throw an assembly off-balance and leave them hanging in mid-air. If the assembly does not know when to say their proper response because the presider has changed the cues, in effect the presider has deprived the assembly of a rightful part in the liturgical action! Relative to the number of words the presider says in the course of the liturgy, the assembly's parts are minimal. It is all the more important that they be able and encouraged to say everything that is rightfully theirs. The few "Amen's" of the liturgy may seem insignificant, but they are extremely important in meaning, for they allow the local assembly, the microcosmic incarnation of the Christian Church, to affirm (since "Amen" = "I agree" = "Yes, it is true") what the presider has just finished praying, and thus make the presider's prayer their own.

The opening prayer (or "collect") concludes the entrance procession and introductory rites—it does not (of its nature) introduce the readings.

In the Roman liturgical tradition, on Sundays and feasts the same prayer is used to conclude the Office of Readings, Morning Prayer, and Evening Prayer from the Liturgy of the Hours, and as the Opening Prayer at mass. In the tradition, this prayer expresses general sentiments of prayer appropriate for any communal worship service. It can and does refer to any feast of the Church being celebrated that day, and in that sense often appropriately prepares the assembly to hear the Word of God. However, of its nature, it need not directly refer to the readings which follow, and should serve more as a summation of the sentiments of the assembly, gathered in prayer, attentive to God's presence, and mindful of their needs and deficiencies. The newer vernacular missals of Holland and Italy have included new Opening Prayers for the Sundays of the Year which do blend more with the readings assigned for those days, and the official English translating body, the International Commission on English in the Liturgy (ICEL), is presently working on similar English-language prayers. Even so, these new prayers will still serve as general gathering prayers, whose language is inspired by the readings which follow, not as prayers which introduce the readings per se.

Beware of unofficial prayers.

The following is a quotation from a well-known bishop, writing about some of the prayers he found his priests using:

> The prayers of many are being corrected every day, once they have been read by the learned, and much against catholic faith is found in them. Many blindly seize upon prayers composed not only by unskilled babblers but even by heretics and use them because in their simple ignorance they cannot evaluate the prayers and think them good.

The bishop was St. Augustine (354-430), and he was referring to prayers used to bless baptismal water.[8] But the same sentiments can be expressed concerning prayers one hears today, particularly in adapted liturgies. The prayers in the Sacramentary are not perfect, but at least no one's faith will be led astray by them. That is not necessarily true with prayers found elsewhere, or those composed by members of a committee, or those which the presider prays extemporaneously.

NOTES

(1) *Ritus servandus in Celebratione Missae:* II-De Ingressu Sacerdotis ad Altare, sec. 2.

(2) e.g. Rite for Distributing Communion Outside of Mass, #27.

(3) cf. *Notitiae*, the semi-official journal of the Congregation for the Sacraments and Divine Worship, which reprints many of the newly composed texts for papal liturgies.

(4) Keifer, *To Give Thanks and Praise*, p. 109.

(5) Kavanagh, *Elements of Rite*, p. 77.

(6) Champlin, *The Proper Balance,* pp. 81–82.

(7) cf. Bishops' Committee on the Liturgy [BCL] *Newsletter,* v. 10, ##6–7 (June-July, 1974), pp. 428–29.

(8) Augustine, *De bapt. contra Donastistas,* 6.47; quoted in Allan Bouley, O.S.B., *From Freedom to Formula,* p. 165.

Section 6

THE LITURGY OF THE WORD

Use only one lectern/pulpit/ambo for proclaiming all and only the Word of God.

All contemporary liturgical writers emphasize the importance of ONE lectern/pulpit/ambo from which ALL and ONLY the Word of God is read and nothing else. If another lectern is used (by musicians or commentators or even the presider), it should be significantly different. This is not merely the preference of liturgists—it is found in nearly all major documents and contemporary liturgical writers.

For example, in *Environment and Art* we read:

> A very simple lectern, in no way competing or conflicting with the main ambo . . . can be used by a cantor, song leader, commentator, and reader of the announcements.[1]

The U.S. Appendix to General Instruction of the Roman Missal tells us:

> The reservation of a single place for all the biblical readings is more significant than the person of the reader, whether ordained or lay, whether woman or man.[2]

In the Sacramentary (GIRM #272, DOL-1662), we find:

> It is better for the commentator, cantor, or choir director not to use the lectern.

The 1981 *Introduction to the Lectionary* presents the following comments for our consideration:

45

32. There must be a place [for proclaiming the Word of God] in the church that is somewhat elevated, fixed, and of suitable design and nobility. It should reflect the dignity of God's word and be a clear reminder to the people that in the Mass the table of God's word and of Christ's body is placed before them.

33. Either permanently or at least on occasions of greater solemnity, the lectern should be decorated.

34. In order that the lectern may properly serve its liturgical purpose, it is to be rather large, since on occasion several ministers must use it at the same time.

Dr. Ralph Keifer writes this:

The Sacramentary indicates a preference for using a single lectern. On special occasions (especially for the reading of the Passion), special arrangements can be made. Proclaiming the Word from one place (most of the time) makes the Word prominent in the arrangement of the worship space, a space which communicates a sense of priorities in worship. The Word will lose its prominence if the lectern is the same size as the music stand, or if the sanctuary says in its arrangement that the Word is unimportant and can be proclaimed any old place, or even if the lectern looks like an appendage to the altar. It is just as appropriate and just as desirable to place candles or flowers near the lectern as it is to place them near the altar . . . Just as the Lectionary should not be a repository for notes, as the chalice and paten are not used as cruet holders, neither is the lectern the place for making announcements or leading music. The lectern should be reverenced by using it for its holy purpose—proclaiming the Word—just as the altar is reverenced by not using it as a lavabo towel rack or a stand for a portable font.[3]

In a number of churches two lecterns have been set up on either side of the altar, and the presider uses one of the lecterns or the altar for his part of the mass, while the lay reader uses the other. On the other hand, the Sacramentary directs that only the liturgy of the word should take place at the lectern (GIRM #272, DOL-1662) and only the liturgy of the eucharist at the altar—the presider should remain at his seat for the entrance rites and concluding rites (also see section 4). If another "choreography" is being followed, it is usually because the liturgical judgment is being made based on something else—where the microphones are rather than whether it is good liturgy. In keeping lecterns separate for priest and laity, we are also symbolically saying that it is more important to keep clergy and laity separate than to show forth the unity of God's Word.

Never proclaim God's Word from disposable missalettes or typewritten pages.

In the 1981 *Introduction to the Lectionary* we read (#37):

> Because of the dignity of the word of God, the books of readings used in the celebration are not to be replaced by other pastoral aids, for example, by leaflets printed for the faithful's preparation of the readings or for their personal meditation.

Frequently pastors and people are caught in a mutual bind—readers are so poor that no one in the assembly can truly understand the proclamation of God's Word, so the church must be filled with missalettes. But that is no excuse for using the missalettes by the ministers of the Word. To read God's "two-edged sword" from a disposable missalette is like putting the Blood of the Lord into paper cups—most Catholics would be aghast at the latter but do not bat an eye at the former. Yet in the realm of symbol, both are equivalent. The Word of God is present in the Bread and Wine of the Eucharist and the containers we use for the Sacred Bread and Precious Wine should mirror our faith in Christ's presence. But the Word of God is also present in the Scriptures proclaimed and we attest to that presence by using physical books indicative of our belief in the importance of God's Written Word in our lives. Nothing less will do.

One might also reflect on why we are not more sensitive to reading God's Word from an appropriate book. Once again, this may be a situation of *ex opere operato* still reigning supreme.

Since the words said are the same, whether they are printed in a magnificent, well-bound gospel book, or a newspaper print missalette, the "how" aspect is overlooked. In addition, the Catholic bias to seeing the only "real" presence of Christ as that which is in the eucharist, causes our sensibilities to demand well-made and artistic chalices and plates encrusted with jewels, but at the same time to ignore the equally "real" presence of Christ in Scripture! (I do grant, however, that the scriptural real presence is of a theologically different category than the eucharistic real presence, but both are still *real*).

Never handle the lectionary as if it were a novel.

Especially in smaller liturgies, there is a temptation to "conveniently" put the Book of Readings somewhere where it is "out of the way," which often means on the floor or under a chair. Once again, the equivalent action would be to put a ciborium still filled with consecrated hosts under a chair or on the floor. We would shudder at the latter, but we frequently see nothing wrong with the former. The Byzantine tradition is the Book of Gospels always remains on the altar until it is used for the actual proclamation. Many lecterns are being constructed with a "throne" for the Lectionary, so that immediately after use, it may be placed where it can be reverenced for what it contains—God's Holy Word. Yet, how often does one see a homilist put his notes on top of God's Word—or take the Holy Words and put them in an insignificant place, so that his human words can take their place? This might be considered by some as being tantamount to arrogance (if we look at it on the symbolic level). This seemingly minor action should not be overlooked either, since it deals with a basic symbol of the liturgy—God's presence in scripture and how we physically handle the visible scriptures. Liturgy is basically about helping each other find God's presence in the symbols which surround us, a long and oftentimes tedious process! Thus we should not downplay one of the more obvious liturgical symbols of that divine presence.

Never hide the book of God's Written Word.

The Lectionary is the "chalice" of God's Written Word, and should be handled as such. Just as the chalice and paten are held high at the end of the eucharistic prayer, so the Lectionary and Gospel Book should be held so that the congregation sees them and accepts them as the symbols for what they contain—God's nourishment for a Holy People. In particular, it is better to hold the Lectionary or Gospel Book when reading from it at the lectern so that it may be seen by the assembly, rather than leaving it semi-hidden on the lectern. It may rest on the lectern when not actively being used, but when it is used for the proclamation, it should be visible as the Sacrament of God's Presence. And, as a fitting conclusion to the reading, it should be held high in reverence, while the reader proclaims (after a momentary pause): "This is the Gospel [Word] of the Lord"!

Priests should not read the non-gospel readings if lay readers are available.

Both the Sacramentary (GIRM #66, DOL-1456) and the Lectionary (1981 Introduction, #51) re-iterate a liturgical tradition concerning the ministry of readers. It is a proper function which differs from the function of leadership belonging to deacon and priest. Therefore, even if there are many deacons and priests available, the reading of scripture (except for the gospel) should be done by lay readers.

The response to the first reading must be a psalm (or its liturgical equivalent).

We are frequently put into a no-win situation: the response to the first reading should be sung—but one does not easily obtain singable psalm texts. Therefore, there is a tendency to choose an "appropriate" song as a substitute. Sometimes, these appropriate songs are even based on scripture, but are not from the psalter.

This practice, besides being illicit, is less than ideal and should be discontinued.

It is permitted to use an alternate psalm in lieu of the psalm given in the Lectionary for a given day, but the alternate must be from the Psalter (or its liturgical equivalent, e.g. the Magnificat, the Benedictus, some other Old Testament canticle, as the Song of Hannah). In context of the structure of the liturgy of the word, we (i.e. the assembly) use God's Word to respond to God's Word. Thus the texts should be from Scripture.

And our response should be a true *response*. The psalms were meant to be sung by an assembly in praise of the God of Israel. The wording is such that the psalm addresses God directly (Ps 51—Have mercy on me, O God), or is an exhortation to the self (Ps 104—Bless the Lord, O my soul) or to others to praise God (Ps 95—Come, let us worship the Lord). Using other sections of scripture may seem to fit in with the "theme," but, as a way of enabling the assembly to give voice to the Lord, they are problematic, since, at times, some of these songs quote God addressing his people. This results in a somewhat odd situation where the assembly is using God's exhortation to them and addressing that exhortation back to God.

Presiders should make sure that other ministers perform their ministry well. In particular, make sure that readers always help the assembly with the psalm response.

An amazing number of readers never help the assembly respond to the psalm, by repeating the psalm response audibly. It is as if they are oblivious to the fact the majority of the assembly does not have the text of the response in front of them. The reader of the psalm should both proclaim the verses in such a way that the assembly knows when to answer (normally dropping the tone of his or her voice at the end of each verse), and help them by vigorously proclaiming the response whenever the assembly is supposed to proclaim it. Most of the responses are not all that difficult to remember, yet they are not totally remembered after merely one try.

Never recite the alleluia!

In the Sacramentary (GIRM #39, DOL-1429) we read, "If not sung, the *Alleluia* or the verse before the gospel may be omitted."

But practice has shown that *not* omitting the Alleluia leads to insipid "Acclamations of Joy!" which are neither acclamatory nor joyful. As a result of reflection on merely-recited Alleluias, the 1981 *Introduction to the Lectionary* has eliminated the option and flatly states (#23),

> The *Alleluia* or the verse before the gospel *must be sung* and during it all stand. It is not to be sung only by the cantor who intones it or by the choir, but by the whole congregation together.[4]

The Presider should never read the Gospel if another priest or deacon is present.

The Sacramentary gives us this principle (GIRM #34, DOL-1424):

> Since by tradition the reading of the Scriptures is a ministerial, not a presidential function, it is proper that as a rule a deacon or, in his absence, a priest other than the one presiding read the gospel.

This is also repeated in the 1981 *Introduction to the Lectionary* (#49).

When present, a deacon seeks and receives a blessing from the presider, but another priest does not,[5] unless the presider is a bishop.[6]

Some presiders suggest that since they will deliver the homily, they should also proclaim the gospel because of its intimate connection. It is true that the homily should be intimately connected with the scripture which precedes it, but this principle would suggest that the homilist should proclaim *all* the scripture which is referred to in his homily, not merely the gospel. Proclaiming the *message* of Scripture by giving a homily is a presidential function, but proclaiming the *text* of Scripture by reading a pericope from the Lectionary is a ministerial function. These two actions should not be confused and one way of keeping the roles separate is to insist that the presider never proclaims the gospel if another priest or deacon is present.

Never bow to the tabernacle, when reciting the preparation prayer before proclaiming the gospel.

If no other deacon or priest is available, then the presider himself proclaims the gospel, and the rite prescribes that he should prepare himself by reciting a prayer inspired by Isaiah 6:7. The Sacramentary (GIRM #93, DOL-1483) prescribes that the presider should bow TOWARDS THE ALTAR while reciting this prayer. However, frequently one sees presiders bowing toward the TABERNACLE instead, as if it were "more reverential" to bow before the reserved Sacrament. Besides being contrary to the rubrics, this action puts more emphasis on the reserved Sacrament than good liturgy suggests should be done. The reserved Sacrament should be seen as the fruit of the eucharist—therefore it is inconsistent to "interrupt" the liturgy to make reverence to the reserved Sacrament. As mentioned before, the 1984 edition of the *Ceremonial for Bishops* (#49) directs that if a bishop must celebrate at an altar on which there is a tabernacle, the Blessed Sacrament should be *removed* during the liturgy. During the liturgy, the altar is the primary architectural symbol of Christ, and must be reverenced as such.

Do not omit gesture at the gospel.

Since the gospel is the climax of the Liturgy of the Word, special gestures and postures have been traditionally used to enhance this special Word. The assembly stands. The minister and assembly cross themselves on the forehead, lips, and heart. The minister reverences the text with a kiss at the end. In the Russian and Greek usages of the Byzantine Rite and at papal liturgies after the Greek proclamation of the gospel, the assembly is blessed by the presider with the Gospel Book. All these gestures help the assembly focus on the specialness of the gospel, and as mentioned above, involve the assembly in body-worship as well as mind-worship. Thus, the omission of any of these gestures should not be undertaken lightly!

It is preferred that the homily be given from the chair.

The 1981 *Introduction to the Lectionary* re-iterates an ancient tradition in #26: "The priest celebrant gives the homily either at the chair, standing or sitting, or at the lectern." This emphasizes a tradition which was observed by bishops but overlooked by others—that delivering a homily is part of the office of presiding, and thus should be delivered at the place where the presider presides—the chair. Also following an ancient episcopal tradition, the presider may sit while delivering the homily.

Do not begin or end the homily with a sign of the cross.

In the early 1970's, this question, along with whether it is appropriate to use a greeting to the assembly to begin the homily, was posed to the Congregation for Divine Worship. The answer given was:

> . . . generally speaking it is inadvisable to continue such customs because they have their origin in preaching outside Mass. The homily is part of the liturgy; the people have already blessed themselves and received the greeting at the beginning of Mass. It is better, then, not to have a repetition before or after the homily.[7]

Do not give a sermon, but rather "break the bread of the word" with a homily.

A sermon is a holy speech, a sacred oration—but, of its nature, it need not be connected to scripture. A homily should start
with the context of the celebration, particularly the feast being
celebrated, or, if there is no feast, the experience of the scripture
just proclaimed. It should be a holy reflection on the scripture,
"breaking the bread" of God's Written Word for the assembly so
that they can be nourished by it. It should offer practical appli-
cations to the contemporary experience, and a challenge to the
way lives are lived in the contemporary culture. It is not an aca-
demic lecture containing absolute truth as perceived by the homilist, but a humble sharing of God's graces and insights for the
building-up of God's Priestly People. Most authors suggest that,
ideally, the homily should be only around 7–10 minutes long on
a typical Sunday, and 4–6 minutes long on a weekday. A special
occasion might be able to tolerate a homily of 12–14 minutes.
However, homilies of longer than 15 minutes are usually an imposition on the psyches of members of the assembly. In addition,
oftentimes, "homilists" who go longer than 15 minutes have not
really said anything that could not have been said in the first five
minutes anyway. Some homilists have a bad habit of multiplying
words so that (both they and) the assembly do not realize that
there is no real substance![8]

Do not change the structure of the General Intercessions.

Individuals seem to have a very difficult time understanding
the paradigms given in the Sacramentary for the General Intercessions (Prayers of the Faithful). There are four main sections: *Introduction* by the PRESIDER, *Invitations of Concern* (i.e.
"PETITIONS") by the DEACON, CANTOR, or READER, *Response of
Prayer* by the ASSEMBLY, *Final Concluding Prayer* by the PRE-
SIDER.

Note some of the implications of this structure: (1) The PRE-
SIDER ALWAYS introduces and concludes this part of the liturgy—

it should not be delegated to another priest, or worse still to the deacon or reader. (2) The PRESIDER NEVER offers the invitations of concern (i.e. "petitions") unless no one else who is competent is present. (3) The so-called "petitions" are invitations to prayer—they are statements addressed TO THE ASSEMBLY inviting them to pray for specific topics of concern. In themselves these "petitions" are NOT PRAYERS addressed to the FATHER or to JESUS! (This also holds true for the introduction by the presider—it is NOT a prayer to God. It is rather a statement to the assembly, inviting them to join in prayer for the intentions which will be proposed.) The "prayer" is said by the assembly together, and usually is "Lord, hear our prayer."[4] What frequently happens when the "petitions" are re-worded into mini-prayers to Christ, is that we are left with a series of grammatically incorrect statements—half of each "petition" is addressed to the Lord and the last half "let us pray to the Lord" is addressed to the assembly. The assembly is barraged with a series of schizophrenic statements. No wonder they frequently don't know how to react!

Do not change the intercessions to prayers of thanks.

Sometimes, one hears petitions which read something like, "For Mary and Joe, IN THANKSGIVING for all they mean to us, let us pray to the Lord." Although this somewhat retains the general form for an intercession, this basically states a motive for thanksgiving, and thanksgiving belongs during, or before the eucharistic prayer.

Do not over-localize the intercessions.

Especially in small groups, the petitions can become so localized, praying for intra-community concerns, that one can forget that the local community is part of a wider church. The General Intercessions provide an opportunity for the local church to reach out to the Church Universal in prayer, in concern, and (one would hope) in action.

Remember that the Intercessions are basically a litany.

The General Intercessions form a litany, and litanies are meant to be sung in a mantra-like style inducing an ambience of prayer. Paying more attention to the "how" of the Intercessions (i.e. singing them), than to the "what" (i.e. the text) may produce marvelous and unexpected results!

NOTES

(1) *Environment and Art,* #74–75.
(2) GIRM, U.S. Appendix, comments on section #66c.
(3) Keifer, *To Give Thanks and Praise,* pp. 120–121.
(4) BCL *Newsletter,* v. XXI (October, 1985), p. 39.
(5) 1981 *Introduction to Lectionary,* #17.
(6) 1984 *Ceremonial of Bishops,* #74, 173.
(7) cf. *Notitiae,* v. 9 (1973), p. 178, DOL-1432: note R8; *Fulfilled In Your Hearing: The Homily in the Sunday Assembly,* note 7.

(8) cf. also *Fulfilled In Your Hearing.*

Section 7

THE LITURGY OF THE EUCHARIST

Do not ignore the four-fold biblical structure of the liturgy of the eucharist!

In the narratives of the Last Supper found in the synoptic gospels and Paul (1 Cor 11), in the narrative of the miracles of the multiplications of the loaves and fishes, and in the Post-resurrection appearances of the Lord (e.g. Emmaus), we again and again find the meals described using four verbs: TAKE, BLESS, BREAK and GIVE/SHARE. These four actions shape the liturgy of the eucharist in all liturgical families. Yet in the liturgy of the eucharist, we *do not dramatically re-enact* the Last Supper scene, but rather *liturgically remember* what occurs and incorporate the verbs into the structure of our worship. This last point is more important than it looks. Since the four verbs are so prominent in Scripture, we cannot totally overlook them and still claim to be in continuity with the tradition. Yet these four verbs structure our worship, but not in a way that the eucharistic liturgy becomes a dramatic re-enactment of the Last Supper, as was done in the plays "Godspell" and "Jesus Christ, Superstar."

What has happened in the Christian liturgical tradition, is that TAKING has given rise to the procession with the gifts and their preparation and placement on the altar, BLESSING has given rise to the eucharistic prayer, BREAKING has been preserved in the breaking of the bread rite, and SHARING becomes the reception of communion. To telescope two of these rites together is to do damage to the structure of the liturgy (e.g. to break the bread during the eucharistic prayer). Similarly, not to give proper emphasis to one of these rites is also to do damage to the structure of the liturgy (e.g. to downplay or hide the breaking of the bread). In ad-

dition, to change the nature of the rite is, once again, to do damage
to the structure of the liturgy (e.g. TAKING, BREAKING, SHARING are
actions, NOT words—therefore one should not turn the reception
and preparation of the gifts into a series of "Offering" prayers
since this would be turning an action [taking] into words
[prayers]).

Never plan on distributing hosts from the tabernacle at Mass—or, correlatively—always consecrate enough bread and wine to distribute to those present.

An examination of the various documents issued over the last
20 years reveals an interesting fact. Nowhere is it explicitly mentioned that it is allowed to distribute hosts already in the tabernacle at mass!

All the documents mention the necessity of reverence before
the reserved Sacrament, of how it is lawful and encouraged to
pray before the tabernacle, of how it is permitted to distribute
Communion *outside of mass* from the tabernacle for those unable
to participate in mass (therefore implying that it is NOT permitted
to distribute immediately before or after mass), and of how it is
necessary to reserve the Sacrament for the sick and the dying.
However, whenever referring to the reserved Sacrament, no mention is ever made of distribution during mass.

In fact, the opposite is true. Starting at least back in 1742 we
hear that the faithful should receive Communion from the elements consecrated AT THAT MASS.[1] This exhortation was quoted
by Pope Pius XII in his encyclical *Mediator Dei* in 1947,[2] repeated
in the Vatican Council's Constitution on the Liturgy in 1963,[3] repeated in the Roman Instruction *Eucharisticum Mysterium* in
1967,[4] repeated in the 1969 General Instruction of the Roman
Missal,[5] and also repeated in various other decrees since then! It
should also be noted that this practice was actually urged by the
1570 missal as well![6]

This does not mean that one can never use what is in the tabernacle in distributing Communion at mass. But it does mean that
our planning should be such that we count and plan properly, and

that what is in the tabernacle should be used solely (primarily) as a focal point for prayer and as a resource for the sick. Thus, as a general rule, there should NEVER be more than one container (ciborium) of hosts in a tabernacle, and NEVER be more than about 50 hosts therein. Since in most churches, mass is celebrated daily, that supply for the sick could easily be renewed within 24 hours! This may seem like an obvious rule, but a common older mindset was that mass was mainly to refill the tabernacle, and thus that the tabernacle should always be filled with hosts. Unfortunately for good liturgy, this practice is still in vogue in some parishes!

Do not *offer* the gifts during their *preparation*—in particular, do not lift them high in the air.

The present Order of Mass significantly changed what formerly occurred between the readings and the eucharistic prayer. Now the gifts are received, prepared, and placed on the altar while the priest briefly thanks God for his gifts. Formerly, we "offered" bread and wine to God, but now we realize that offering anything other than Christ is theologically inappropriate and that the real "offering" takes place during the eucharistic prayer, after the institution narrative and memorial acclamation.

There is a significant change in the gestures prescribed by the rubrics as well, which many presiders still have not noticed (cf. GIRM #102, DOL-1492). The Tridentine Missal required the presider to hold the paten and chalice at eye-level in a gesture of "offering," while looking at the corpus on the altar cross. The present Sacramentary omits the looking at the corpus for two reasons: first of all, the "altar" cross need not have a corpus, and, secondly, since it MUST be seen by the assembly, but not always by the priest, the cross can be on the back wall of the sanctuary, behind the presider! In addition, the Sacramentary speaks about holding the gifts "slightly" above the altar. The Latin word used here is *aliquantulum*, the same word used in the old missal to describe how high the presider held the chalice up during the former "minor elevation," i.e., the doxology of the eucharistic prayer.

In many rubrical books, this was interpreted as "3–4 inches"[7] or "a hand's breadth."[8]

This brief examination of the revised rubrics in the previous paragraph helps shed a bit more light on the present structure and purpose of this part of the liturgy. It is primarily a receiving of the bread and wine from the people, briefly thanking God for these gifts, and only then placing them on the altar. We are trying to retrieve the ancient simplicity of this part of the liturgy. Originally, the gifts were accepted from the people and (in one sense) received an initial "sanctification" by simple contact with the altar—the basic architectural symbol of Christ (cf. Mt. 23:19–20 where Christ indicates that the altar makes holy the gifts placed on it). Thus, we do NOT OFFER—that will be done during the eucharistic prayer. We also should not have the gifts on the altar already—that is counter-symbolic since they should touch the altar only *after* the prayers are said.

Practically, an ideal choreography might go like this. The priest receives the gifts of bread and wine from the people and gives the wine to the deacon or server (the water should be on the credence and not brought up since it is a non-biblical [yet ancient] addition to the "matter" of the eucharist). The presider continues to hold the vessel with the bread and quietly says the appropriate prayer while slightly holding the vessel over the altar, and only after the prayer does he let the vessel with bread touch the altar. Meanwhile, at the credence, the deacon (or concelebrant) pours the wine *and water* into the chalice and holds it for the presider until needed. Once again, only after the appropriate prayer does the chalice touch the altar. If there is no deacon or concelebrant, it is possible (although somewhat awkward) for the presider to prepare the chalice himself at the credence, or to hold the chalice off the altar at the side while pouring the water and wine into it. What should be avoided is the common senario where the gifts are placed on the altar at the center once, then lifted up at eyes' level while the prayers are said, then placed on the altar again, as if the prayers were the most important point of this section of the liturgy.

To re-iterate, it is better to prepare the chalice at the side table—this should be done by the deacon or concelebrant (and *not* the Presider). In addition, the water is *not* blessed.

The Sacramentary (GIRM #133, DOL-1523) makes a note that the deacon may prepare the chalice at the side table *saying the accompanying prayer*, and in view of the historical meaning of the gifts touching the altar—the symbol of Christ—in general this seems to be a better practice. Note that the deacon (or concelebrant) should pour *both* the wine *and the water* into the chalice. The sign of the cross, *blessing the water,* required in the Tridentine Mass, *is omitted* in the present Sacramentary.

Do not prepare the gifts while the collection is being taken.

This is basically a warning against another example of doing two things at the same time. The collection is part of the gathering of gifts for the celebration. Some of those gifts consist of bread and wine which will be "eucharistized" through the prayer voiced by the presider. Some of those gifts might also consist of specific food offerings for the poor, especially on days like Thanksgiving. Usually, some of the gifts consist of monetary offerings used for the basic necessities of community life, such as paying utility bills and salaries. All of these items are gifts of the community to be presented to the presider of the community for the benefit of the community. It is improper to accept some gifts and prepare them at the altar while the other gifts are still being gathered.

Do not make a habit of saying the "offertory" prayers aloud.

Close examination of the rubrics of this point of the liturgy reveal that the first option given in the Sacramentary is for ALL the prayers (including the two "BLESSED ARE YOU, LORD . . ."

prayers) to be recited *quietly* by the presider. Then the Sacramentary gives the option that IF there is NO SINGING, the presider MAY (but is *not* required to) say the two "BLESSED ARE YOU . . ." prayers aloud. If these two prayers are recited audibly, then the assembly MAY (but again is *not* required to) respond with "Blessed be God forever."[9]

This part of the liturgy corresponds to the biblical action of TAKING—which is ACTION, NOT WORDS. Thus, it is *not* primarily a time for words. In fact, the words can be counter-productive in that they can take away from the important words which follow—the eucharistic prayer.

Reciting ALL the prayers audibly, rather than just the two "Blessed are You . . ." prayers, makes all the prayers seem of equal value. Therefore, members of the assembly cannot sense, from what they hear, what is primary and what is secondary.

Do not clutter the altar with unneeded ciboria and chalices.

Altars can sometimes look like awards tables at bowling banquets,[10] or like vendors' tables at pottery crafts shows. We need the strong symbol of ONE BREAD and ONE CUP. If more than one container is needed because of the quantity of bread and wine needed for the assembly, then the plate should be expanded to be able to contain all the bread needed, and one cup can be augmented by one (or more) large decanters, carafes, or flagons. This is a new rubric in the latest edition of the Italian Missal[11] and is also mandated by the Directory for Communion under Both Kinds for the United States.[12]

Do not wash your fingertips—wash your hands.

In the 1965 revision of the rubrics, the phrase which suggested that all the presider had to do when he "washed his hands" was merely wash the thumb and index finger of both hands, was omitted. Similarly, in the present Sacramentary, the rubric simply says that the presider should wash his hands (GIRM #106, DOL-1496).

The general canonical principle is that when some law is changed in this manner, the older practice is meant to be changed. The older practice was in the spirit of Roman minimalism, and the truth of the sign and symbol is that HANDS should be washed—not merely FINGERTIPS. Thus, this also necessitates "finger bowls" big enough to be able to properly wash hands in, and "finger towels" which can be used to dry HANDS, and not merely fingertips!

It is not uncommon to see this rite omitted, either occasionally or regularly, something not generally permitted by the rubrics except occasionally in Masses with Children. The washing of hands in the Roman Rite finds its origin as a *practical* necessity following the presider's acceptance of gifts from the people, and then incensing them. It is unknown in many other major liturgical families. However, it has now taken on the added *symbolic* meaning of renewing one's baptismal purification, appropriate before offering the sacrifice of praise. Thus, if performed with meaning, it can help the assembly to appreciate the connection between the purifying waters of baptism and the celebration of the eucharist. Therefore, its omission should not be done lightly, as if no other alternatives are possible!

The Prayer over the Gifts concludes the preparation rite—it does not introduce the eucharistic prayer.

The Prayer over the Gifts is basically the final prayer which summarizes the second major procession of the liturgy—the procession with the gifts. It corresponds to the Opening Prayer which ultimately concludes the Entrance Procession, and the Prayer after Communion which concludes the Communion Procession. This prayer is introduced by the "Pray, Bethren . . ." now interpreted as an elongated form of "Let us pray" (in fact, in the German Missal, the simple "Let us pray" is given as one of three options to introduce the Prayer over the Gifts). This prayer should mention "offering" only insofar as the gifts have been received and placed on the altar for the "Offering" which is the Sac-rifice of Praise vocalized in the eucharistic prayer and ratified in the reception of Communion. To re-word or amend the prayer texts to turn the Prayer over the Gifts into an independent "offer-ing"-prayer, or an independent "epiclesis"-prayer invoking the Spirit, is to detract from the eucharistic prayer as the primary place where such sentiments rightfully are expressed in the tra-dition of Christian Eucharistic Worship.

Since, as mentioned above, the "Pray, brethren . . ." is now viewed as an elongated "Let us pray," the presider should *not* say "Amen" after the assembly's response, "May the Lord receive . . ." This practice is either a mis-reading of the rubrics in the present Sacramentary (which says that the *assembly* responds with "Amen" after the Prayer over the Gifts), or a continuation of the custom prescribed in the Tridentine Missal.

Follow the rubrics regarding each of the eucharistic prayers.

In particular, eucharistic prayer II should not normally be used on Sundays (since GIRM #322b, DOL-1712b, specifically mentions its use is "suited for weekdays"), and eucharistic prayer IV (along with the eucharistic prayers for reconciliation) should not be used with any preface other than the one written as part of it (cf. GIRM #322d, DOL-1712d).

Do not interrupt the eucharistic prayer for announcements.

This seems logical enough, but the preliminary problem rests with understanding what really constitutes the eucharistic prayer. The eucharistic prayer begins with the introductory dia-logue of the priest ("The Lord be with you" . . . "Lift up your hearts") and ends with the final "Great" Amen of the assembly after the doxology ("Through him . . ."). Unfortunately, many people still think of the eucharistic prayer as being two parts (i.e.

the Preface with the Holy, Holy, and the "Canon"), and many people act as if it were four parts (i.e. Preface with Holy, Holy; Consecration section up to [AND including] the memorial acclamation; Memorial section up to [but NOT including] the final doxology; the Final Doxology and Amen). As a result, one sees the unity of this most important of all the prayers of the Mass constantly being compromised. For example, many presiders will announce, AFTER the Holy, Holy, which "eucharistic prayer" they are using, even though they are already part-way through the eucharistic prayer. Similarly, at concelebrations, after the memorial acclamation, the principal celebrant will have only one of the concelebrants (illegally) read the next section of the prayer (i.e. the anamnesis and communion-epiclesis). Or, frequently there is a significant time gap between the end of the intercessions and the beginning of the doxology while the presider is getting the paten and chalice in his hands and even inviting the assembly to "join me in reciting the 'Through him.' " Any of these practices destroys the sense that the eucharistic prayer is ONE prayer (albeit with several different parts).

If an announcement is necessary it should occur BEFORE the preface dialogue. It should be noted that this is one of the places mentioned in the Sacramentary (GIRM #11, DOL-1401) and the Directory for Masses with Children (#22, DOL-2155) as appropriate for the presider to give a brief admonition (and invite the assembly to think of motives for thanksgiving)![13]

Never break the host at the words of institution.

Breaking the host during the eucharistic prayer while saying "He broke the bread, gave it to his . . ." telescopes together two distinct actions in the Liturgy of the Eucharist—blessing and breaking—and tries to turn liturgical remembrance into dramatic re-enactment. In addition, it is not even correct dramatic re-enactment, since, by almost every theology around, the bread is not really "blessed" (i.e. consecrated) until AFTER the point at which certain presiders break it. This practice, therefore, instead of imitating scripture more closely, actually reverses the order found therein (i.e. BLESSING, BREAKING is turned into BREAKING, BLESS-ING).

Father Aidan Kavanagh is very strong in his dislike of those who break the host at an incorrect time. He writes the following:

> The president of the assembly is not a mimic whose task is to reproduce the Last Supper. He is a servant who serves the assembly in its celebration of the eucharist by proclaiming in its midst the motives for which it gives thanks. That on the night before he died, Jesus took bread, said the blessing, broke and gave it to his friends is a central motive for the assembly's giving thanks to God, but, as the eucharistic prayer itself makes clear, it is not the only one. The eucharist is not a mnemonic tableau of an historical event. It is a sweeping thanksgiving for the whole of the Father's benevolence toward the world and his people in Christ and the Holy Spirit. It does no more than what Jesus did in all the meals he took with those he loved. What he did at those meals quite escaped the bounds of any one meal on any one occasion. What he did was to make human beings free and forgiven table partners with God. Mimicking the details of what Jesus did at only one of those meals thus historicizes a mystery which transcends time and place, saying in the process far too little rather than too much. Christian liturgy is not an historical pageant. Presidents who cannot be convinced of this should not preside.[14]

Dr. Ralph Keifer agrees with Father Kavanagh's perceptions:

> Breaking the host at the institution narrative is an abuse because the narrative is mainly a recital of why we celebrate the Eucharist (because this is the way the Lord Jesus has given us to regularly share together and celebrate his presence and power to transform us), not a demonstration of what we do at Eucharist. If the narrative were a demonstration of what we do, it would be appropriate not only to break the bread, but also to eat it at that point, and, the words having been said over the cup, to share that at this point also. The institution narrative is not designed to be a liturgical show-and-tell. It is designed, rather, to say that we celebrate the Eucharist because it is the memorial of the Lord.[15]

It might also be pointed out that it is conjectured by some that very early eucharistic prayers did not have the institution narrative within the eucharistic prayer. Thus, it would have been impossible for them to break the bread at that point. The Canadian *Bulletin* several times reminds presiders to follow the rubrics and not to think that moving the breaking of bread leads to better liturgy.[16] For some reason, this seems to be a wide-spread phenomenon for which there is no justification among any of the writings of liturgical experts.

Be careful about what is done with the doxology of the eucharistic prayer.

The doxology of the eucharistic prayer is still part of the presidential prayer, and thus should be proclaimed by the presider alone (although at concelebrations, the concelebrants *may* join him, but are not obliged to do so, cf. GIRM #191, DOL-1581). That this section of the eucharistic prayer is the sole domain of the presider was re-iterated by the 1980 Instruction *Inaestimabile Donum* which states (#4): "The doxology itself is reserved to the priest." This is preceded a few sentences earlier by the statement, "It is therefore an abuse to have some parts of the eucharistic prayer said by the deacon, by a lower minister or by the faithful."[17]

However, in spite of this statement, it is a common practice for some assemblies to join the presider (sometimes at his invitation) in reciting the doxology. Practically, this tends to trivialize the Great Amen to a whisper, yet it does help many in the assembly feel that they are adequately affirming the eucharistic prayer. In addition, at least among the Maronite Rite Catholics from Lebanon, the final phrase of the doxology of the eucharistic prayer ("now and always and forever") is communally recited, indicating that the practice is in the realm of liturgical possibility. In addition, the Maronites also communally recite a doxology during the breaking of the bread which immediately follows the eucharistic prayer and precedes the Lord's Prayer.

Nevertheless, all things being equal, in the Roman Rite, the presider should not invite the assembly to join him in reciting the doxology (since it does break up the unity of this presidential prayer), and instead should foster efforts to enhance the Great Amen which follows.

If there is an assisting deacon (or concelebrant), he should hold the chalice during the doxology. The presider always holds the *bread* (cf. GIRM #135, DOL-1525).

One final comment pertains to the height of the gifts during the doxology. Some scholars have found ancient texts which indicate that this is the high point of the eucharistic prayer—theoretically and physically/visually. This is the major "physical" elevation. This is the point for the visible "offering," the point at which the gesture of offering gifts to heaven found in the Hebrew Scriptures should be imitated. Unfortunately, many presiders are still under the impression that the height prescribed in the Tridentine Missal (a few inches) should be continued now. The contrary is true. Although nothing is specifically mentioned in the Sacramentary, evidence suggests that the doxology is the time for the grand gesture of lifting high the gifts toward heaven for all to see.

Do not trivialize the "great" Amen.

St. Jerome and other early authors mention the importance of the concluding Amen to the Eucharistic Prayer, and how it sounded like thunder in the city of Rome, shaking all the pagan temples.[18] However, in most churches nowadays, it is more of a whimper than anything approximating thunder. Oftentimes this is due to the presider's not saying the doxology of the eucharistic prayer in such a way that it elicits a response by the people. Whatever the cause, the problem needs to be cured.

The Presider need not "distribute" the sign of peace to the assembly.

At one point in the development of the Roman Rite mass, the "Peace" was received from the altar by the presider (when he kissed the altar at this point), and then passed to the deacon, who in turn passed it to the subdeacon, etc. The present Sacramentary has tried to abolish this hierarchical "trickle-down" clerical practice in favor of everyone in the assembly exchanging the peace immediately with those closest. There is no sense that the presider is "the sole" minister of peace in the assembly. Yet this is what is symbolized when a presider walks throughout the church, trying to greet someone in every pew. The presider has already greeted everyone via the liturgical greeting, "The peace of the Lord be with you always." He need not greet anyone aside from those around him, except in special circumstances (e.g. weddings, funerals). To do elsewise tends to unreasonably prolong this section of the liturgy and obscure the fact that "TAKING" and "BLESSING" should *soon* be followed by "BREAKING" and "SHARING."

Do not ignore the breaking of the bread.

The Lamb of God accompanies the *significant action* of the breaking of the bread. The breaking of the bread does NOT accompany the *insignificant recitation* of the minor litany: "Lamb of God . . ." In other words, what is important is that the Breaking of the Bread be seen by the assembly as a section of the liturgy as important as the preparation of the gifts, the eucharistic prayer and the distribution of Communion. In Luke's gospel and the Acts of the Apostles, we have direct references to the "Breaking of the Bread" with eucharistic implications. This action is of immense significance! However, one often sees presiders who sneak the breaking of bread in while the Kiss of Peace is still continuing. Such a practice leads to a poorer experience and understanding of sharing in the one bread and one cup for all present. In addition, it should be noted that striking the breast during the Lamb of God is no longer required, and thus should be omitted.[19]

The Presider must personally distribute Communion.

One of the key functions of the presider is to proclaim the eucharistic prayer, and, by implication, this includes the action intimately related to the reason for the eucharistic prayer—distributing the Sacred Elements.[20] The 1980 Instruction *Inaestimabile Donum* also calls into question the practice which does occur here and there, of the presider sitting during the Communion of the faithful while lay ministers take over "the unimportant task, which the priest doesn't really have to do." Actually, the Instruction is very strong in saying (#10) "a reprehensible attitude is shown by those priests who, though present at the celebration, refrain from distributing Communion and leave this task to the laity." Distributing Communion is neither unimportant, nor is it a function of presbyters and deacons that can lightly be delegated to laity. It is a task intimately connected with their function in the liturgy of the eucharist. It continues their role in the Church as primary ministers of God's mysteries.

Do not change the rite of distributing Communion to make it more efficient and less personal.

In some places, seemingly in the interests of efficiency "self-intinction" is or has been practiced for Communion under both kinds. No major liturgical writer has ever suggested that intinction is a good way to distribute Communion under both kinds—drinking from the cup is always to be preferred. "Self-intinction" forces all communicants to take a host themselves and then to dip it in the chalice. Also, this practice does not give people the option of receiving Communion on the tongue, and we must respect that piety even if we disagree with it. In addition, this practice eliminates the necessity for a minister in the action of receiving Communion, therefore de-personalizing it, and turning an action which for centuries has been seen as "humbly receiving God's gifts," into "taking what is rightfully mine."

Father Robert Taft, S.J., an expert on the liturgies of the Eastern Christian Churches, writes:

> But from the sources we have studied at least one thing is clear: the eucharist, ideally at least, is not something one *takes*. It is a gift received, a meal shared. And since sacraments by their

very nature are supposed to symbolize what they mean, then self-service, cafeteria-style communion rites just will not do.[21]

This same re-orientation of symbol takes place anytime the sacred elements are passed through the congregations, as frequently happens in some small group liturgies.

Father Robert Hovda writes:

> The personal sharing and transaction between minister and communicant is part of the symbolic action. That is why it is such a loss when that personal dimension is eliminated by the use of a mode of sharing which does not involve a minister of the plate and a minister of the cup. One sees this not infrequently: plates simply passed through a group, or cups simply placed on the altar to be found by communicants. The loss is not a minor one. It is a loss of personal eye contact, personal word, personal gesture, personal touch.[22]

If the group is small enough, it may be a very meaningful adaptation, once in a while, to pass the elements among all the people present, but to do that in a larger group, forcing everyone in a non-homogenous group to "take" rather than "receive," in the minds of most liturgical authors, results in a poorer liturgical experience.

Be sensitive to unimportant clerical-lay or male-female local "traditional" distinctions when arranging Communion ministers.

In some parishes, only priests or deacons minister the bread, and the laity minister the cup. Elsewhere, one sees men with the bread and women with the cup. Should these distinctions be kept at Communion time? Traditionally, the presider ministers the bread and the deacon the cup, but when auxiliary lay ministers are used, there should be an equal mix (and an alternating mix) at the various Communion stations with men and women having an equal opportunity to minister either species.

Do not purify the vessels at the center of the altar. Do so at the side of the altar, or (even better) at the side table, or (ideally) wait until after Mass.

The American Directory for Communion under Both Kinds (*This Holy and Living Sacrifice*) makes a distinction between *consuming* the left-over species and *purifying* vessels. Any left-over Precious Blood is to be consumed *immediately* after Communion (#36), and Consecrated Bread is to be stored in a tabernacle. However, the Sacramentary indicates a *preference* for purification after Mass ("especially if there are several vessels to be purified"—GIRM #120, DOL-1510), at the credence table ("if possible at a side table"—GIRM #238, DOL-1628).[23] If it seems absolutely necessary to purify immediately after Communion at the altar, the priest should NEVER stand at the center of the altar, but rather *at the side*.[24]

Do not have a litany of 'thanksgiving' after Communion.

For a few years after the present Order of Mass was introduced, it was popular to fill in the silent meditative period after Communion with a "Litany of Thanksgiving." However, reflection on the practice has led liturgists to see this as less than ideal. The key moment for "thanksgiving" is the eucharistic prayer, and if there are particular items that need to be announced as reasons for special thanksgiving, they would most appropriately be mentioned immediately *before* the preface dialogue of the eucharistic prayer (NOT after Communion and also NOT during the General Intercessions). After Communion may be an appropriate time for a hymn of praise, but "a litany of thanksgiving" focuses energies away from the primary time of thanksgiving during the liturgy.

Do not make announcements before the prayer after Communion, thereby turning it into a preliminary blessing.

I grant that it is more convenient to make announcements when everyone is seated and quiet. However, announcements do damage to the flow of the liturgy if done before the Prayer after Communion. The post-Communion quiet is a period of reflection after encountering the Risen Christ through eating and drinking his body and blood in Communion. The Prayer after Communion concludes this reflection and concludes the Communion procession, thereby also concluding the entire Liturgy of the Eucharist. The announcements (which regulations demand should be *brief*) are made to remind the assembly of significant major items, not lists of minutiae which can be read in the parish bulletin—those minutiae have nothing to do with Communion. They are looking out from the liturgy toward other activities—thus they should precede the final going-out which is the purpose of the concluding rites.

NOTES

(1) cf. *Certiores effecti*, sec. 3, #5 ff.

(2) *Mediator Dei*, #121.

(3) Constitution on the Liturgy #55, DOL-55.

(4) *Eucharisticum Mysterium*, #31, DOL-1260.

(5) GIRM #56h, DOL-1446h.

(6) cf. also Canadian *Bulletin*, v. 9, #54 (May-June, 1976), p. 174; v. 14, #77 (Jan-Feb, 1981), p. 31.

(7) cf. O'Connell, *The Celebration of Mass*, p. 234.

(8) cf. Mueller, *Handbook of Ceremonies*, p. 84.

(9) cf. BCL *Newsletter*, v. 8, ##7–8 (July-Aug, 1972), pp. 334–35.

(10) cf. Canadian *Bulletin*, v. 14, #77 (Jan-Feb, 1981), p. 8.

(11) cf. BCL *Newsletter*, v. XX, ##4–5 (April-May, 1984), p. 16.

(12) cf. *This Holy and Living Sacrifice*, ##40–43.

(13) cf. *Eucharistiae Participationem*, #8, DOL-1982.

(14) Kavanagh, *Elements of Rite*, pp. 74–75.

(15) Keifer, *To Give Thanks and Praise*, p. 140.

(16) cf. Canadian *Bulletin*, v. 9, #54 (May-June, 1976), p. 160, note 9; v. 14, #77 (Jan-Feb, 1981), p. 16.

(17) cf. also note R37 to GIRM #191 in DOL-1581.

(18) Jerome, *In Epist. ad Galat.* 2, *praef.,* PL 26:381.

(19) cf. DOL-1477, note R22.

(20) cf. Hovda, *Strong, Loving and Wise,* p. 36.

(21) Taft, "Receiving Communion—A Forgotten Symbol?", p. 418.

(22) Hovda, in Kay, *It is Your Own Mystery,* pp. 31–32.

(23) cf. also GIRM #138, DOL-1528.

(24) cf. clarification regarding GIRM #238 in *Notitiae,* v. 14 (1978), pp. 593–594; translation in *Liturgy Documentary Series* 2, pp. 111–112 and in DOL-1628: note R42.

Section 8

THE CONCLUDING RITE

Do not change the Presider's role by "blessing us" rather than "blessing you."

This may be a point of great debate, but the topic should be raised because at least one noted liturgist sees significant implications when the formula for the final blessing is slightly altered so that the presider says "May almighty God bless *us* . . ." instead of "May almighty God bless *you* . . ." What can be so important and so significant about changing a pronoun from second person to first person? Isn't the presider part of the assembly? Shouldn't God's blessings be sought for him also? Yes, the presider is part of the assembled Christian community, and yes, God's blessings should be sought for him also. However, this does not necessarily imply that in his role of presiding over the assembly he should not call God's blessings upon others and exclude himself, similar to the way that parents traditionally bless children, or to the way that the patriarchs of the Hebrew Scriptures blessed others.

In a 1975 issue of *Living Worship,* Father Robert Hovda connects the re-wording of the final blessing to the whole issue of presidential style (or lack of it). We read:

> Without any desire to emulate them, we can sympathize with those priests who seem to shrink from the task of presiding at liturgical celebrations. We see them dropping out of sight whenever possible. We see them evidently embarrassed by their occupying a chair in our full view, or by the vesture that they wear with studied carelessness (as if to say "these things don't matter"). *We see them refusing the role by turning "you" to "us" in blessing, thus avoiding the personal confrontation so essential to good liturgical experience.* We see them forsak-

ing any trace of reverential dignity for the sake of a nervous, giggly, phony chumminess. We see them presiding as if not presiding—in other words, rejecting their role of service.[1]

Albeit, Father Hovda seems to put the full weight of good presidential style on one pronoun in the blessing, but the implications that such a change makes in the liturgy as a whole are much broader than most people would suggest.

Do not bless "in the name of" the Father, etc.

As a priest, I absolve "in the name" of the Father, etc., and I baptize "in the name" of the Father, etc. However, I do not ask God that God should bless "in the name" of the Father, etc. God *cannot* bless "in the name" of anyone—God blesses "directly." The Latin version of the blessing is slightly clearer as to *what* is being expressed—unfortunately a literal translation leads to less than ideal English: "May [he] bless you, [he who is] almighty God, [that is] Father, and Son, and Holy Spirit." Using this statement, the presider is *not* blessing (in the name of anyone). Rather, the presider is asking that God (Father, Son and Spirit) bestow his blessing on the assembly.

Do not omit "the Lord be with you" when using solemn blessings or prayers over the people.

Although the text of the greeting, "The Lord be with you" is not printed in the Sacramentary, the rubric printed there says that *the greeting* should be given by the presider before the deacon says, "Bow your heads . . ." and then the Solemn Blessing is pronounced.

NOTES

(1) Hovda, "The Eucharistic Prayer Is More Than Words," *Living Worship*, v. 11, #4 (April, 1975), p. 2 (emphasis added).

Section 9

VARIA

TOPIC 1—CONCELEBRATION

Concelebration is a liturgical rite and not a devotional practice.

Concelebration is a liturgical option. In this sense, it is similar to other options available, like the choice of the eucharistic prayer. Whether the option is chosen or not should depend on pastoral considerations.[1] The rubrics accompanying the three eucharistic prayers for children flatly state that children's masses should *not* be concelebrated (a directive I personally am not completely comfortable with).[2] In some liturgical families (i.e. the Byzantine Rite), all concelebrants must be at the altar for the eucharistic prayer (at least ideally); thus it is sometimes necessary to limit the number of concelebrants. On the other hand, at least theoretically, the Ethiopian Rite *requires* about 5 concelebrants (preferably 7 and ideally 13) if the eucharist is to be celebrated at all![3] The standard rubrics for a Pontifical liturgy in the Byzantine Rite *requires* the bishop to have at least one concelebrating priest. Symbolically, this binds the bishop to working with his priests, even in the celebration of the eucharist!

In the present day situation in the Western Church, concelebration is required only at ordinations, and is prohibited only at children's liturgies. At other times, whether a concelebration is permitted and whether a given priest chooses to concelebrate is left to the judgment of the appropriate authority and the devotion of the individual priest. In the typical situation in the Western Church, especially in cases where there is no deacon, a concele-

77

brant can often aid the total liturgical experience, by proclaiming the gospel, assisting at the altar, ministering communion. Therefore, I personally would always encourage concelebrations rather than having priests celebrate "private" masses or attending mass *modo laico* (as a lay person). This does not mean that all priests present must concelebrate, however, and sometimes, other concerns (such as avoiding liturgical "mob" scenes, avoiding a male-dominated liturgy, preserving a balance between "ministers" and "assembly") might suggest that it would be appropriate to limit the number of concelebrants.[4]

However, concelebration for many priests, particularly members of religious institutes, is a way of "getting mass in," while avoiding saying a private mass. It is true that the official documents encourage concelebration,[5] but the reasoning given in the documents seems to be because of the sign value of the unity of the Church—not because of the personal devotion of the priest. This distinction is important because, if taken seriously, it can influence the way various concelebrations may take place. It is the assembled Church which should be the primary beneficiary of the liturgical rite—not primarily the devotion of the individual concelebrant.

Concelebration is not a committee presidency.

Any arrangement of concelebrants which reminds people of the board of directors versus the stockholders of a corporation should be avoided. Only one presbyter can preside. Other presbyters present may concelebrate, and if they do, they liturgically function as needed to serve the entire assembly. They do not co-preside. Rather, they co-celebrate (as every baptized Christian present does) according to their presbyteral rank. Co-celebrating (according to their presbyteral rank) means that they can join in imposing hands over the elements and in QUIETLY reciting the central section of the eucharistic prayer. This also means that they join in consecrating the elements. However, this does not mean that they are equal in liturgical function to the principal celebrant. The principal celebrant leads all present—including the concelebrants. In many respects concelebrating priests are more a part of the assembly of the faithful than they are leaders of worship. Only the principal celebrant recites the presidential prayers—only he should give the homily (although on special occasions, it may be appropriate for a concelebrant to give the homily).[6]

Concelebrants should be seen, but not necessarily heard.

The rubrics insist that the volume level of the concelebrants, especially during the eucharistic prayer, should be "quiet" (GIRM #170, DOL-1560).[7] All the priests present do not act as if they were one huge Greek chorus. They should be seen, however. During the eucharistic prayer, they should be near the altar, but NOT at the altar (GIRM #167, DOL-1557). The gesture of imposition of hands during the invocation of the Spirit is the ONLY required gesture by a concelebrant and should normally be made with TWO hands (cf. GIRM #174a et passim, DOL-1564a). The gestures at the words of the Lord are optional (cf. GIRM #174c et passim, DOL-1564c).[8]

The principal celebrant should be heard!

Many principal celebrants have the bad habit of lowering their voice during the common section of the eucharistic prayer. This makes it more awkward to concelebrate, since the concelebrants cannot usually hear the principal celebrant if he reduces his voice to a whisper. The requirement that all concelebrants recite the central sections of the eucharistic prayer is there in the present rite solely to satisfy the demands of present theology (many people would suggest that this practice is actually bad liturgy). A concelebrated proclamation of the eucharistic prayer should never be a Greek chorus type of proclamation. The presiding celebrant must also preside during a concelebration and lead the concelebrating presbyters in prayer. To do this he must be 'heard! In general, the principal celebrant should actually raise his voice during the common section to make sure he is heard both by the concelebrants, and also by the assembly during this most important of all prayers (cf. GIRM #170, DOL-1560).[9]

The principal celebrant should not have two assistant chaplains, unless he is a bishop, in which case the two chaplains should be two deacons.

At many concelebrations, one frequently sees three "major" concelebrants seated together. This practice is probably an unconscious imitation of the old "three-priest solemn high mass" with a bit of the "chaplains to the bishop" thrown in for good measure. Nowhere is it ever suggested that a simple priest needs any assistants or chaplains at a concelebration. Concelebrants should all be seated together, APART from the principal celebrant. If assistance is needed because of a lack of other qualified ministers (deacons and acolytes), one or more of the concelebrants may help at the appropriate time, but they should not be seated together with the presider.

Only in the case where the principal celebrant is a bishop should there be "chaplains" seated on either side of him, and it is preferable that these chaplains be deacons, NOT concelebrating priests![10]

Do not delegate the anamnesis (memorial) section of the eucharistic prayer to only one concelebrant.

The Sacramentary (and Introduction to the Eucharistic Prayers for Reconciliation) requires that *all* concelebrants together recite (quietly!) the eucharistic prayer from the consecratory epiclesis (invocation) through the consecration and anamnesis (memorial) to and including the communion epiclesis (GIRM #174, DOL-1564 et passim). This section constitutes a "bare-bones," "mini-"eucharistic prayer containing *all* parts common to all eucharistic prayers (and which are considered "essential" by many authors). Thus, according to present Roman Rite discipline, a concelebrant must recite all of his part (i.e. the entire "mini-"eucharistic prayer) to concelebrate licitly. Merely reciting the first half (up to the words of Christ), or merely reciting the Words of Consecration is not enough to satisfy the rubrics (and also for ecumenical concerns).

I should also note that some renowned scholars (Karl Rahner, S.J. being one of them) have questioned the necessity of any co-vocalizing of sections of the eucharistic prayer.[11] However, until there is an official change in rubrics, all concelebrants must recite the memorial (anamnesis) and communion invocation (epiclesis) sections *after* the consecration as well as the invocation before.

On the other hand, it is not necessary to delegate any of the eucharistic prayer to concelebrants. A presider may want to proclaim the entire prayer himself, and some authors suggest that this is actually a better liturgical practice.[10]

The basic symbol of the eucharist is *one bread and one cup*. Therefore, only one plate and one cup should be elevated at the doxology.

There is a bad habit which has the two concelebrating "chaplains" to the presider elevating two chalices while the presider elevates the bread. This seems to be done for the sake of symmetry (the same reasoning for having two "chaplains"). But this custom is based on a non-liturgical reason (i.e. "symmetry" or "balance"). The correct practice is for the presider to hold the vessel of bread and the *deacon* (or *one* concelebrant, if there is no deacon) to hold *the* chalice (since there should only be one chalice on the altar anyway) (cf. GIRM #135, DOL-1525). This correct practice once again highlights the fundamental symbol of the eucharist—*one bread and one cup.*

TOPIC 2—FUNERALS

Do not begin twice.

The American funeral rite begins with the reception of the coffin at the door of the church. The rite of reception is the formal beginning of the Mass—the usual penitential rite is omitted (along with the sign of the cross) and the greeting should be done at the door of the church, preceding the sprinkling and clothing of the coffin. When the procession reaches the sanctuary, the presider continues with (a simple welcome to those present on behalf of the family of the deceased and then) the opening prayer.

Never turn the homily into a eulogy.

The Sacramentary specifically forbids a eulogy at a Catholic funeral (GIRM #338, DOL-1728). However, it continues to be a common occurrence to hear praises of the deceased as if the funeral were actually a canonization rite. The homily must be based on scripture, but also should not neglect the life of the particular Christian that died. It should encourage the assembly to a deeper faith in eternal life, based on the faith of Christ who found life through his own death on the cross. The presider should not ignore the connection between the death of a Christian and the death of Christ, and thus fail to use the funeral liturgy as a faith-building experience for the local Christian assembly.

The Rite of Christian Burial does allow a family member to say a few words before the final commendation, at the end of the liturgy. This may be an appropriate time for a few familial remembrances, but again, it should not turn into a list of reasons for canonizing the deceased.

Do not end twice.

The Funeral Mass ends with the "Amen" responding to the Prayer after Communion. The Concluding Rite *is omitted* (i.e. the

Blessing and Dismissal), and *in its place,* the Final Commendation and Farewell take place.

Do not turn the farewell into a series of 'absolution' prayers.

· The rite of commendation and farewell after the Prayer after Communion has a very simple structure: Invitation to Farewell, Song of Farewell, Concluding Prayer, Recessional. The ritual *tolerates* merely-recited invocations ONLY IF THERE IS NO POSSIBLE WAY TO SING AN APPROPRIATE 'FAREWELL' SONG. The main point of this rite is to bid farewell in song to the deceased—it is *not* an "absolution," trying to add more prayers to the greatest prayer possible—the eucharistic prayer! The introduction to the funeral ritual states that this hymn should be experienced as the climax and high point of the entire funeral rite.[13] Unfortunately this section of the liturgy is usually experienced as a strange mixture of quasi-magical rites (water and incense), unknown responses (who remembers the exact wording of "Saints of God, Come to His Aid"?), and more wordy prayers. This is NOT good liturgy (besides being illegal!). Appropriate "Farewell" Hymns can be found in contemporary hymnbooks, set to tunes which can be used even with most heterogeneous funeral congregations.[14] If a hymn is actually sung as the rubrics require, the additional 'tolerated' petitions are to be OMITTED, since they should only be used when no singing is possible!

NOTES

(1) cf. 1983 Code of Canon Law, canon 902.

(2) Introduction to the Eucharistic Prayers for Children, #22, DOL-2020.

(3) Taft, "Ex Oriente Lux?", p. 310.

(4) cf. Archbishop Hunthausen, "Male and Female God Created . . .", Pastoral Recommendations #7, "We will continue our effort to avoid male dominance in liturgical settings . . . by us-

ing care concerning the appropriateness of concelebrations . . .";
cf. also BCL Study Text 5, *Eucharistic Concelebration,* section V,
pp. 19–23, "Concelebration is never presented . . . as a way of
dealing with large numbers of priests . . . there are occasions
when the number of concelebrants will need to be limited . . ."

   (5) cf. *Eucharisticum Mysterium, #47,* DOL-1276.

   (6) cf. also BCL Study Text 5, *Eucharistic Concelebration;*
BCL *Newsletter,* v. XVI (November, 1980), pp. 234–35; also cf.
Baldovin, "Concelebration."

   (7) also cf. footnote R36 at DOL-1558.

   (8) also cf. footnote R36 at DOL-1558.

   (9) also cf. footnote R36 at DOL-1558.

   (10) cf. *1984 Ceremonial of Bishops, #26,* 128.

   (11) cf. J. McGowan, *Concelebration,* pp. 77 ff.

   (12) cf. Smolarski, *Eucharistia,* pp. 140–41.

   (13) Introduction to Rite of Funerals, #10, DOL-3382.

   (14) e.g. "Song of Farewell" in *Peoples Mass Book* (1984 edition) (#748); also see Appendix; also cf. 1985 Order of Christian
Funerals, 396 E, 403 #5, and The Liturgy of the Hours: Office
for the Dead, Evening Prayer, Alternate hymn.

Section 10

WHAT TO DO?

In his poem, "To a Louse," Robert Burns gives us these often quoted words:

O wad some Pow'r the giftie gie us
to see oursels as others see us!

Along with the thoughts of Burns, for our consideration let us add the following paraphrase of a verse from Our Lord, as recorded in the gospel of Matthew (Mt. 13:9):

Those who have *eyes* to *see* with,
let them *see*.

Much improvement can occur in our lives and our liturgies if we somehow can remove our blind spots and see our imperfections the way others do.

Now that this book has been read (or skimmed), what should a presider do to improve a liturgy, or what should a liturgy committee do to help the presiders in their parish improve the parish liturgies? I wish there were a simple answer to this question—the author of the answer would be canonized for a great contribution to the spiritual life of the Church, besides becoming a millionaire in this life! But there is no simple answer. In some cases, helping others improve their liturgies may be as difficult as trying to teach willing and hopeful teenagers how to be great actors—the willingness is there, but the techniques need much development. However, some suggestions may be helpful.

First of all, priests who have been ordained for a number of years might risk having themselves videotaped during a typical mass, or even a special "dry" mass. Videotaping is a technique in common use in many seminaries today as part of a liturgy training class for prospective priests, and certainly it would be a rare parish in which at least one family did not own their own portable television camera and VCR. In seminary courses, after a taping of a "mass," one or more professors and one or more contemporaries criticize the "presider" and make suggestions, both to point out rubrics whose spirit or letter were not quite fulfilled, but also to help the future presider become more natural, more human in gestures, in the same way that an actor is helped by a drama coach to become more natural in a dramatic role. The same critique can also be accomplished without a television camera, but videotaping has the advantage of letting the presider "see ourselves as others see us" if he has "eyes to see with" as the poem and scripture go.

Another suggestion for veteran priests is to visit other churches and "attend" mass, primarily to learn from another presider what may or may not be helpful in leading others in prayer. It is a rare occurrence for some priests to be at a mass presided by another. This experience may be an eye-opener to some. (Why is he doing that? Could I be wrong?) To others, it may be excruciatingly painful. (Will this awful homily *never* end? I wonder if I preach that poorly?)

In order to improve gestures (and other aspects of style), one suggestion given by a seminary professor in a "How To" liturgy class was that future presiders "say mass" in front of a full length (or full wall) mirror *without* any words, and try to let their *gestures* and *body-language* do the "talking." A critique based on this technique can be very enlightening. Did a specific gesture convey the meaning of the unspoken text? Why or why not? How can this be improved? (One can also do this via videotape by turning off the sound!)

Finally, it may be good for each presider, once a year, to re-read the *General Instruction of the Roman Missal* and the detailed rubrics in the Order of Mass to recall what he should or should not be doing. Once we get ourselves into a pattern, it is hard to break it, even if it is incorrect. However, the worship of the Lord and the service of God's people deserve our best efforts.

The rubrics of the Sacramentary are like a recipe for a fine pastry. Following or ignoring the rubrics (or the recipe) will not automatically guarantee success or failure. But overlooking basic principles can lead to disaster—one does not substitute salt for sugar just because they look the same.

This book is an attempt to help presiders and all who work with the liturgy become more sensitive to authentic liturgical traditions as found in the present Roman Rite. Following the suggestions presented here will not automatically guarantee a "perfect" mass nor will it eliminate all problems. But becoming sensitive to the principles behind the suggestions presented here may help all of us realize that worship of our God is more than minimally correct actions and an avalanche of words. It is a human interaction, an affair of the heart, a combined effort of all believers who are assembled together, each leading the others to a deeper love of the Divine Lover and to a deeper commitment toward one another, as they share the Bread of Life and the Cup of Eternal Salvation.

APPENDIX

The following are two versions of the Song of Farewell, as given in the Rite of Christian Burial. Both are translations of the old Latin Hymn, *Subvenite,* and are set to two different, but standard musical meters, and thus they can be sung according to various commonly recognized melodies. [Italicized pronouns should be changed in gender and number as the situation requires.]

METRICAL VERSION A—LONG METER

Come to *his* aid, O saints of God;
Come, meet *him,* angels of the Lord.
Receive *his* soul, O holy ones;
present *him* now to God, Most High.

May Christ, who called you, take you home,
and angels lead you to Abraham.
Receive *his* soul, O holy ones;
present *him* now to God, Most High.

Give *him* eternal rest, O Lord.
May light unending shine on *him.*
Receive *his* soul, O holy ones;
present *him* now to God, Most High.

(Optional additional verse)
I know that my Redeemer lives,
the last day I shall rise again.
Receive *his* soul, O holy ones;
present *him* now to God, Most High.

Familiar melodies
> 88.88 (Long Meter)
> Old Hundredth ("Praise God, from Whom All Blessings
> Flow")
> O Salutaris Hostia
>
> 88.88.88 (by doubling the last two lines of each verse)
> St. Catherine ("Faith of Our Fathers")
> Melita ("Almighty Father, Strong to Save"—Navy Hymn)

METRICAL VERSION B—COMMON METER

> Come to *his* aid, O saints of God;
> O angels, meet *him* now.
> Receive *his* soul, present *him* now
> to God, the Lord Most High.
>
> May Christ, who called you, take you home;
> Near Abr'am may you rest.
> Receive *his* soul, present *him* now
> to God, the Lord Most High.
>
> Give *him* eternal rest, O Lord;
> May *he* have endless light.
> Receive *his* soul, present *him* now
> to God, the Lord Most High.

(Optional additional verse)
> I know that my Redeemer lives;
> The last day I shall rise.
> Receive *his* soul, present *him* now
> to God, the Lord Most High.

Familiar melodies
> 86.86 (Common Meter)
> Amazing Grace
> St. Anne ("O God, Our Help in Ages Past")
> St. Flavian ("These Forty Days of Lent")

BIBLIOGRAPHY

Baldovin, John F., S.J. "Concelebration: A Problem of Symbolic Roles in the Church," *Worship*, v. 59, n. 1 (Jan., 1985), pp. 32–47.

Bouley, Allen, O.S.B. *From Freedom to Formula: The Evolution of the Eucharistic Prayer from Oral Improvisation to Written Texts* (Studies in Christian Antiquity, v. 21). Washington, DC: Catholic University Press, 1981.

Certiores effecti, Encyclical letter to the Italian Bishops, Pope Benedict XIV, November 13, 1742.

Champlin, Joseph M. *The Proper Balance*. Notre Dame, IN: Ave Maria Press, 1981.

Directory for Masses with Children, Sacred Congregation for Divine Worship, November 1, 1973.

Documents on the Liturgy: 1963–1979—Conciliar, Papal, and Curial Texts. Collegeville, MN: The Liturgical Press, 1982.

Emminghaus, Johannes H. *The Eucharist: Essence, Form, Celebration*. Collegeville: The Liturgical Press, 1978.

Environment and Art in Catholic Worship, Bishops' Committee on the Liturgy, National Conference of Catholic Bishops, 1978.

Eucharistiae Participationem, Letter to the Presidents of the National Conferences of Bishops concerning Eucharistic Prayers, Sacred Congregation for Divine Worship, April 27, 1973.

Eucharistic Concelebration. Bishops' Committee on the Liturgy Study Text 5.

Eucharisticum Mysterium, Instruction, May 27, 1967.

Fulfilled In Your Hearing: The Homily in the Sunday Assembly.

Bishops' Committee on Priestly Life and Ministry, National Conference of Catholic Bishops, 1982.

Guzie, Tad W. *The Book of Sacramental Basics*. New York: Paulist Press, 1982.

Hovda, Robert W. *Strong, Loving and Wise: Presiding in Liturgy*. Collegeville, MN: The Liturgical Press, 1976, 1980.

Hunthausen, Most Rev. Raymond G., Archbishop of Seattle, "Male and Female God Created . . .": A Pastoral Statement on Women in the Church, October 2, 1980 (excerpts in *Catholic Mind,* September, 1981).

Inaestimabile Donum, Instruction, April 3, 1980.

Kavanagh, O.S.B. Aidan. *Elements of Rite: A Handbook of Liturgical Style*. New York: Pueblo Publishing Co., 1982.

Kay, Melissa (ed.). *It is Your Own Mystery: A Guide to the Communion Rite*. Washington, DC: The Liturgical Press, 1977.

Keifer, Ralph A. *To Give Thanks and Praise*. Washington, DC: National Association of Pastoral Musicians, 1980.

Living Worship. The Liturgical Conference. v. 11, #4 (April 1975).

Mediator Dei, Encyclical letter of Pope Pius XII, November 20, 1947.

McGowan, Jean Carroll, R.S.C.J. *Concelebration: Sign of Unity of the Church*. New York: Herder and Herder, 1964.

Mueller, S.J., John Baptist. *Handbook of Ceremonies: For Priests and Seminarians*. St. Louis, MO: B. Herder Book Co., 1958.

Music in Catholic Worship, Bishops' Committee on the Liturgy, National Conference of Catholic Bishops, Second Edition, 1983.

The Mystery of Faith: A Study of the Structural Elements of the Order of Mass, The Federation of Diocesan Liturgical Commissions. Washington, DC, 1980.

National Bulletin on Liturgy (Canadian Conference of Catholic Bishops).

O'Connell, J. B. *The Celebration of Mass*. Milwaukee: The Bruce Publishing Co., 1964.

Pontificalia insignia, Motu Proprio, June 21, 1968.

Power, David N. *Unsearchable Riches: The Symbolic Nature of the Liturgy*. New York: Pueblo Publishing Company, 1984.

A Reader: The Environment for Worship. Bishops' Committee on the Liturgy, National Conference of Catholic Bishops, 1980.

Regan, Patrick, O.S.B. "Liturgy and the Experience of Celebration." *Worship* v. 47, n. 10 (Dec. 1973), pp. 592–600.

Smolarski, Dennis C., S.J. *Eucharistia: A Study of the Eucharistic Prayer*. New York: Paulist Press, 1982.

Taft, Robert, S.J. "*Ex Oriente Lux?* Some Reflections on Eucharistic Concelebration," *Worship* v. 54, n. 4 (July 1980), pp. 308–325.

Taft, Robert, S.J. "Receiving Communion: the Forgotten Sign," *Worship* v. 57, (1983), pp. 412–418.

This Holy and Living Sacrifice: Directory for the Celebration and Reception of Communion under Both Kinds. National Conference of Catholic Bishops, Nov 1, 1984.

Walsh, S.S., Eugene A. *Practical Suggestions for Celebrating Sunday Mass*. Glendale, AZ: Pastoral Arts Associates of North America, 1978.

The official introductions to the liturgical books can also be obtained in the latest revised editions from various sources.

General Instruction of the Roman Missal [from second *editio typica* of the Roman Missal (1975) with emendations from the 1983 CIC] Washington, DC: USCC, 1982 Publication No. 852 (Liturgy Documentary Series 2).

Lectionary for Mass: Introduction [from second *editio typica* of the Lectionary for Mass (1981)] Washington, DC: USCC, 1981 Publication No. 839 (Liturgy Documentary Series 1).